Creative *felting*

Lizzie Houghton

LARK BOOKS

A Division of Sterling Publishing Co., Inc.
New York / London

Library of Congress Cataloging-in-Publication Data

Houghton, Lizzie, 1948-
   Creative felting / Lizzie Houghton. -- 1st ed.
      p. cm.
   Includes index.
   ISBN-13: 978-1-60059-224-9 (pb-trade pbk. : alk. paper)
   ISBN-10: 1-60059-224-4 (pb-trade pbk. : alk. paper)
   1. Felt work. I. Title.
   TT849.5.H79 2008
   746'.0463--dc22
                                        2007023812

10 9 8 7 6 5 4 3 2 1

First Edition

Published by Lark Books, A Division of
Sterling Publishing Co., Inc.
387 Park Avenue South, New York, N.Y. 10016

First published 2007
Under the title CREATIVE FELTING
By Gaia (an imprint, part of) Octopus Publishing Group Ltd
2–4 Heron Quays, Docklands, London E14 4JP

© 2007 Octopus Publishing Group Ltd
All rights reserved
Americanization © 2007 Octopus Publishing Group Ltd

3987

Distributed in Canada by Sterling Publishing,
c/o Canadian Manda Group, 165 Dufferin Street
Toronto, Ontario, Canada M6K 3H6

If you have questions or comments about this book, please contact:
Lark Books
67 Broadway
Asheville, NC 28801
(828) 253-0467

Manufactured in China

ISBN 13: 978-1-60059-224-9
ISBN 10: 1-60059-224-4

For information about custom editions, special sales, premium and corporate purchases, please contact Sterling Special Sales Department at 800-805-5489 or specialsales@sterlingpub.com.

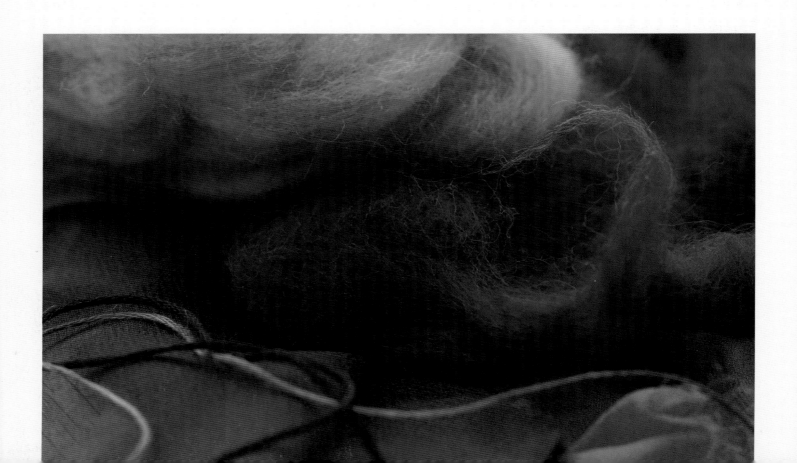

Contents

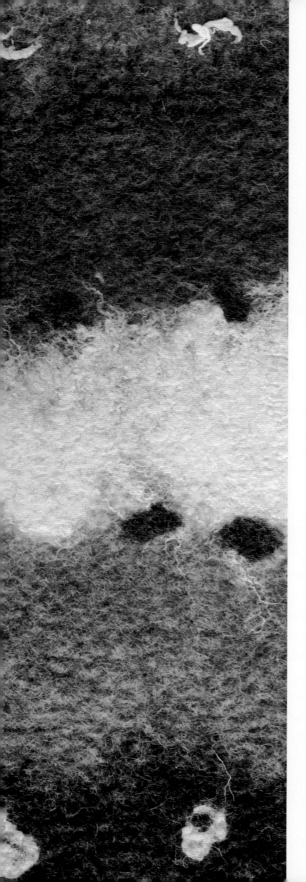

Introduction

Over the last thirty years there has been a great revival in the ancient craft of feltmaking, or felting. The transformation of wool into felt is magical and great fun to do. Anyone can make felt, and for small items it is a very quick and easy process. With knowledge and practice, more complicated pieces may be created. Today's designers and craftworkers are producing some very exciting and imaginative experimental textiles.

The application of heat, moisture, and friction to wool makes it into felt. Each individual wool fiber has scales along its length and when hot water is added, the scales open up. As the wool is manipulated, they begin to tangle with each other. Many of us have inadvertently discovered this by putting a woollen item into the washing machine and ending up with a shrunken, thick, and felted garment.

Felt is believed to be the oldest textile made by Man, dating back to the neolithic period. Because felt is organic, very little has survived from this time. More has been found from the Bronze Age and Iron Age: the most well-known and exciting examples were found in a tomb in the Altai Mountains of Siberia in 1929. An ornate saddle cover and wall hangings reveal highly skilled and sophisticated felting. The colorful work uses techniques such as appliqué, mosaic, and positive and negative inlay.

This book will guide you through the basic felting process and then encourage you to experiment with color, fibers, and fabrics to make sumptuous surfaces and textures. It will stimulate and inspire you, and above all help you to explore your own creativity. Have fun!

How to use this book

The first chapter will show you the simple procedure for making a basic piece of felt. Little equipment is required, and you will already have most of it in your home. This is followed by different techniques that give you the building blocks for turning a straightforward piece of felt into something more intricate, colorful, textured, imaginative – even wild and wonderful. The instructions in the book are for making samples only but, where appropriate, there are suggestions for using the finished felt. Felting is not an exact science: no two pieces of felt turn out exactly the same. Different wools behave in different ways, and factors such as the thickness of the layers of wool also affect the end result.

The remaining chapters contain a series of projects to try. These are inspired by the natural world and grouped by color. You do not have to stick to the listed colors and materials: feel free to choose your own if you wish.

Enjoy experimenting with color and forget – or break – the rules. Look at flowers: examine the contrasting colors around the centers, and the markings on their petals. Marvel at all the different shades and shapes of leaves, and the way that their colors change through the seasons. Be inspired by mosses, lichens, and bark, and their contrasting textures. Let your mouth water at the beauty of fruit and vegetables, taking note of their shape and form, and the seeds and fibers you find when they are cut open. All of these observations and many more will enrich your art and your life.

Materials and equipment

Felting is a great opportunity to indulge a love of color, and the ease with which you can produce stunning pieces is intoxicating. As you immerse yourself in this woolly world, build up a treasure chest of materials to revel in. The equipment list is short and sweet, so you can soon get going.

Materials

Felt is made from sheep's wool, but a variety of fibers can be incorporated into a piece of felt to achieve different textural and decorative effects.

Merino wool

The type of wool most easily turned into felt comes from the merino sheep. Merino wool is popular with felters and is the wool used for the projects in this book. Merino wool is readily available in a myriad of wonderful colors. You buy it after it has been cleaned, processed, and dyed. It is combed and formed into a long, soft rope known as a wool top.

Other types of wool

Some of the projects include wool from different breeds of sheep – the Wensleydale, black Welsh, Jacob, blue-faced Leicester, and fin. Wool and hair from other animals, such as alpaca, angora, camel, cashmere, llama, and mohair can be felted, too.

Other fibers

When you have mastered the basics of felting, you may want to experiment by incorporating other materials into your felt. You can add various natural fibers, such as silk, and flax, for visual and textural interest. These can be either in the form of scraps of fabric, or individual fibers.

Silk fibers come in many different forms, such as silk tops and silk waste, and silk fabrics, such as silk noil (this has small pieces of cocoon woven into it), tussah silk (the yarn has an uneven slub), and douppion silk (yarns are of irregular thickness; the fabric has an uneven surface). The cocoon of the silkworm, and fibers from the soya bean and bamboo, can also be used to create interesting and unusual effects.

Various threads can be stitched into a piece of felt for added decoration. You can use silk thread: either machine or hand embroidery thread, or thread frayed from woven silk fabric, or silk waste (sometimes supplied in thread form). Try shiny rayon machine embroidery thread and stranded cotton hand embroidery thread, too: these are available from craft shops and haberdashers.

Suppliers

You can buy merino wool tops and other types of wool from craft suppliers for weaving, spinning, and felting. They also stock a range of other fibers that you can use for embellishment, and equipment such as carders.

Soap and water

Apart from wool, all you need is hot water and soap. The heat and moisture, plus agitation, cause the wool fibers to mat together; soap helps to speed up the process by encouraging the water to penetrate the wool. Use either a bar of soap or soapflakes (products containing olive oil are kindest to the hands).

So start collecting scraps of natural fabrics, together with natural yarns and threads of various thicknesses and textures, for embellishing felt. This is also a great opportunity to recycle old garments.

Recycled knitting

Many people have inadvertently felted wool knitwear by washing it at too high a temperature. It may be possible to resurrect it as a fashionable felt garment, but you may need to remove the neckband if it has become too tight. Remember that cut felt will not fray or unravel; you could add cuts and slashes. If it cannot be saved as a garment, you can chop it up and use the knitting as a base for felting.

Equipment

The equipment list for felting is not very long. You make felt on a flat surface; it is a wet process, so protection for the surface (and yourself) is required. You could cover a table with oilcloth or even bubble wrap, although the latter may not remain absolutely watertight. You may choose to work in some sort of tray, such as a cat litter tray or a gardening tray, which will contain the water. Alternatively, work on the draining board alongside the sink. Find a waterproof apron, and you may also want to wear rubber gloves.

In addition to the bubble wrap, you can use an old cane windowblind, which provides extra friction, thereby assisting the shrinking process. It also helps to keep the bubble wrap in position. (To use the blind on its own would allow the water to escape and leave the towel drenched from the start.) A reed beach mat could be used instead of a cane blind if you wish. The net curtain is used to keep the wool stable as you add water. Plastic sheeting ensures that the finished felt will be as smooth as possible.

When you make felt, the wool shrinks. The size of the working piece will reduce to produce the finished piece. Decide how big, approximately, you want the finished piece to be: this affects the size of some of the things on the equipment list (see box, right).

To felt you will need:

- **Carders** (optional; for blending colors and fibers, see page 15)
- **Shallow plastic tray**
- **Old towel** (to soak up the water used in the process)
- **Cane blind** with metal parts removed or reed beach mat (optional)
- **Bubble wrap** (twice the size of the finished piece)
- **Piece of old net curtain** (twice the size of the finished piece)
- **Jug or spray bottle**
- **Two pieces of thin plastic sheeting** (each twice the size of the finished piece)
- **Piece of thick dowelling or a rolling pin** (length as for longer side of the finished piece)
- **Plastic bowl**

Basic felting

Decide how big you want your finished felt to be, and select the equipment to suit. You are going to lay out the wool fibers in a rectangle – the working piece. However, the felting process will cause the working piece to shrink and this must be taken into consideration when laying out the wool. The finished piece will be 25–30 percent smaller in each direction, so make an allowance for this.

STAGE 1. LAYING OUT THE WOOL

1 Fold an old towel in half and spread it on the work surface, put the old cane blind or beach reed mat on it, if using, and lay the bubble wrap on top of that, with the bubbles facing upwards.

2 Divide the wool top in half lengthwise. Pull out pieces about 4 in (10 cm) long and place them across the bubble wrap. Each piece should overlap the previous one. This forms the first strip. Make a second strip in the same way. It should overlap the first strip like a row of roof tiles. Continue making further strips until the rectangle is the required dimensions. This completes the first layer.

3 Create a second layer, in the same way, on top of the first – but this time placing the fibers at right angles to the first layer). The second layer should be the same thickness as the first: the first layer may show through the second one but, if working in a different color for each layer, this will add to the texture and quality of the finished piece of felt.

4 If you wish, add a third layer by placing pieces of wool on the second layer at random or in a pattern.

5 Cover the rectangle with a piece of old net curtain. This will prevent the fibers from moving during the felting process.

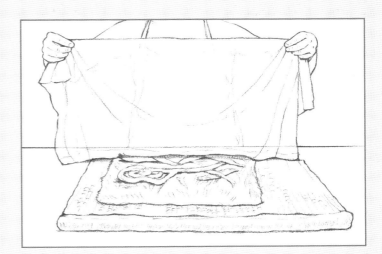

STAGE 2. WETTING OUT

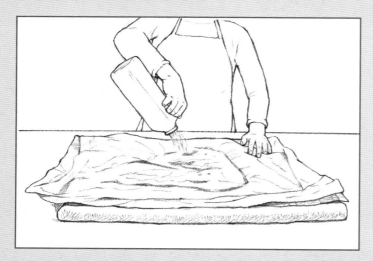

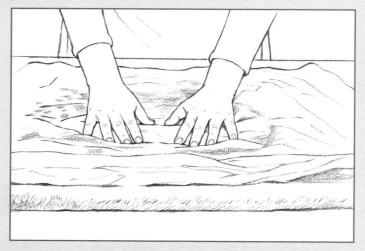

6 Put the bar of soap in a jug of hot water and swish it around until the water is soapy. Remove the bar of soap. The soapy water can be used straight from the jug, or put it into a sprinkler bottle. (Keep the bar of soap at hand for applying extra soap to the felt if necessary. The water does not penetrate the wool fibers easily if there is not enough soap.) Sprinkle or pour the solution all over the surface of the rectangle.

7 Using the flat of your hands, press with open fingers until the wool has compacted and is wet through.

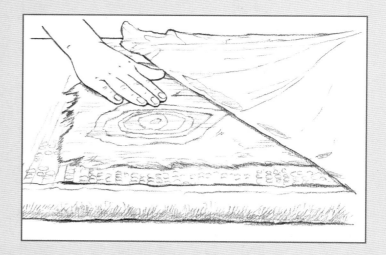

 Tip **A plastic milk bottle with holes punched in the lid makes a good sprinkler utensil.**

8 When the wool is completely wet and flat, remove the net very carefully. Make sure you do not pull off any fibers with the net. Check that there are no dry spots: if there are, wet them.

STAGE 3. FELTING

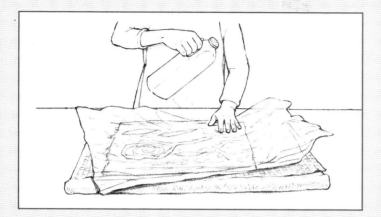

9 Replace the net with a piece of thin plastic sheeting, having wet the surface of the plastic a little with soapy water to make it slippery. Now start the felting process.

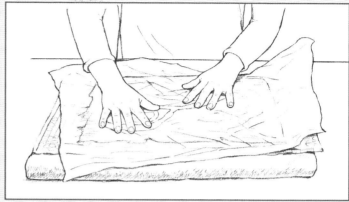

10 Begin rubbing the wool with your hands, through the plastic, to lock the fibers together. Rub in a circular motion. The process may take about ten minutes or more.

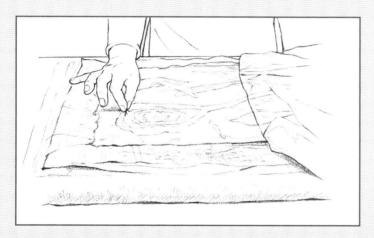

11 Lift the plastic occasionally and pinch the felt between finger and thumb. If any fibers lift up, it isn't ready. Continue until fibers no longer lift up when you apply this pinch test. Supporting the felt on the sheet of plastic, turn the whole thing over. Place the other piece of plastic on top and start rubbing as before. Apply the pinch test again.

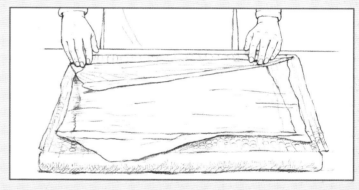

12 Neaten the edges of the felt by folding the plastic over the felt and smoothing it down, as illustrated. Alternatively, soap your fingers and rub the edges into a softer finish.

At this stage you are left with a pre-felt, which is used for appliquéd felt and mosaic work (see pages 16–17).

STAGE 4. SHRINKING

13 The shrinking, or fulling, process comes next. With a piece of plastic sheeting covering the felt, place the dowelling on the long edge of the rectangle and roll up the bubble wrap and the felt as one, around the dowelling, to form a long bundle. Roll it tightly.

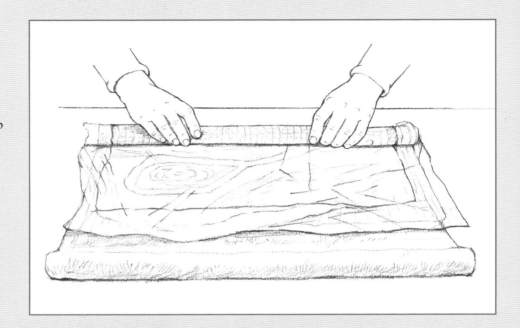

14 Drain any excess water by holding the bundle over the plastic bowl. However, it is important that the felt retains sufficient water for the next task, which is rolling.

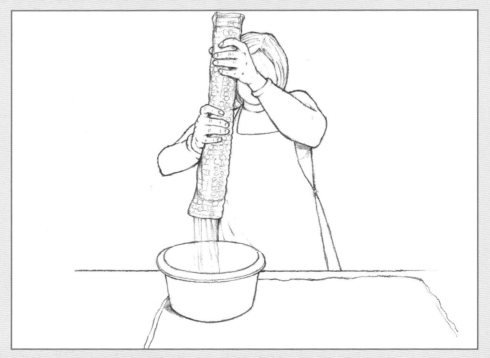

15 Roll the bundle backwards and forwards 20–30 times. If the bundle has become too slippery to roll easily, make use of the towel by wrapping a bit of it around the bundle before you roll it.

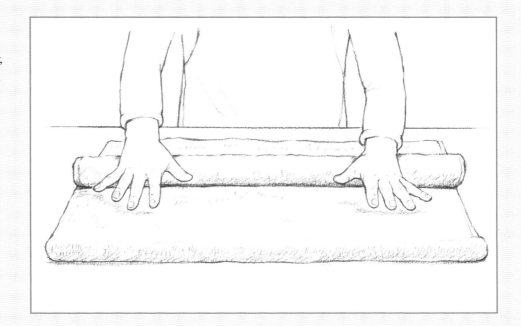

16 Unroll the bundle, turn the felt and the plastic 90°, then roll them up again and repeat the rolling process. Do this several times, turning the felt and plastic 90° each time. It will shrink in both directions and become much thicker. If the felt is going to be put in a frame for display, or hung on the wall, it may be hard enough by now. However, for anything that will receive a lot of wear, such as a cushion or a bag, it is important that it is shrunk as much as possible—otherwise it will pill badly (become covered with small balls of fluff). The felt should end up about 25–30 percent smaller than the size of the rectangle of wool that you laid out at the beginning.

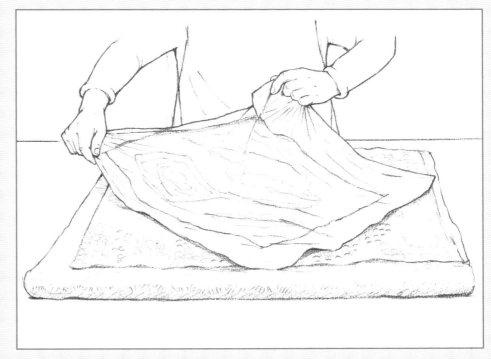

STAGE 5. COMPLETING THE FELT

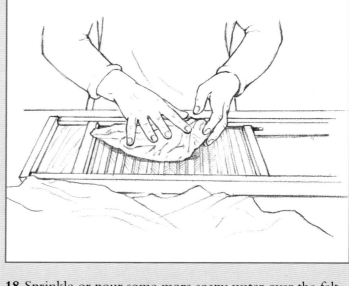

17 After shrinking, unroll the felt. Fill the bowl with very hot water (as hot as your hands can take) and immerse the felt. Remove the felt and squeeze out the water.

18 Sprinkle or pour some more soapy water over the felt and rub it with your hands, on the bubble wrap or against a washboard. The felt will shrink even further. Continue adding soapy water and rubbing until the felt is fully shrunk (when it no longer has any stretchiness to it).

19 Rinse the finished felt in warm water. (For an extra-soft finish, add a few drops of white vinegar to the water. This will neutralize any remaining soap.) The felt can now be pulled into shape and dried. Dry it in any way you wish – in the sun, on a radiator, or place some cotton fabric over it and iron it dry. If you require a very smooth finish, roll the felt again while it is wet, then unroll it and dry it flat.

Techniques

When you have learned how to make a basic piece of felt, set off on a voyage of discovery by trying out some of the exciting techniques here. These will enhance your work and send your imagination scurrying off in all directions.

Blending

BLENDING WITH CARDERS

If you want to blend different colors of wool together before you begin felting, or blend wool with other fibers such as silk, this can be done either by hand or by using special brushes called carders, which can be obtained from craft suppliers for weaving, spinning, and felting. They are easy to use and make a more uniform blend. You can achieve lots of interesting effects by mixing colors that you wouldn't necessarily think of putting together. Experiment—and enjoy the unpredictable results.

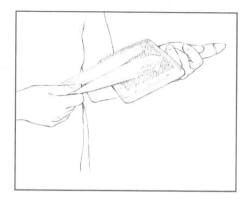

1 Hold a carder with the teeth upright, and place a tuft of each of the fibers to be mixed on the teeth.

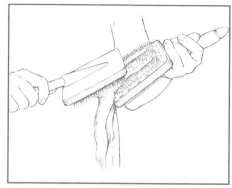

2 With the other carder, teeth pointing downwards and against those of the first carder, gently brush the fibers, moving the carder along to a different place with each new stroke.

Transfer all the wool to the second carder then brush in the opposite direction. Repeat the process until the colors or fibers are mixed to your satisfaction, then remove the wool in a single piece.

Tip

Blending by hand

1 Place the fibers to be mixed in your left hand. Gently pull out fibers from the tips with your right hand.

2 Place these back in your left hand and repeat the process several times until the desired effect has been achieved.

Making pre-felt

Pre-felt is felt that is not fully finished. The wool fibers have been worked sufficiently to have begun to mat together, and the felt is strong enough to pick up without falling apart, but the shrinking process has not been carried out. Pre-felt is used in techniques such as appliquéing and mosaic. To make pre-felt, follow the instructions for basic felting, working to the end of Stage 3 (page 11).

EMBELLISHING PRE-FELT

It is possible to incorporate stitchwork into dry pre-felts before they are used further. Thick, textured yarns or embroidery silks can be worked on the shapes by hand; or use shiny threads for machine embroidery. For further embellishment, small scraps of exotic fabrics could be stitched in, which will distort as the felt is shrunk (see Adding Fabrics and Other Fibers to Felt, page 18).

Appliquéd felt

Appliqué is the technique of applying small shapes of a material to a base material. Make pieces of pre-felt, in the required colors, to cut into shapes and join to a base of pre-felt. Refer to Stages 1, 2, and 3 of the instructions for basic felting on pages 8–11, and to Making Pre-Felt (left).

SHARPLY DEFINED PATTERN

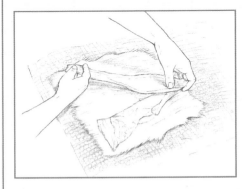

1 For a design that is sharply defined, apply the pre-felt shapes to a pre-felt base and then wet thoroughly with hot, soapy water.

2 Press down hard with a piece of plastic sheeting and finish in the usual way (Stages 3, 4, and 5 of basic felting, pages 11–14).

LESS DEFINED PATTERN

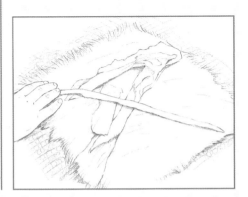

1 For a less defined pattern, apply the pre-felt shapes to wool that has just been layered (Stage 1 of basic felting) and has not yet been wetted or rolled, then continue through Stages 2, 3, 4, and 5, pages 10–14.

Mosaic

A mosaic is made up of individual pieces of pre-felt, which are set out in a design and then bonded into a single piece. This can be a very exciting process. Refer to the instructions for basic felting on pages 8–14, and to Making Pre-Felt (page 16).

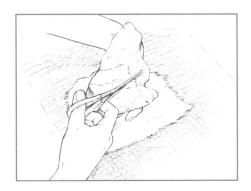

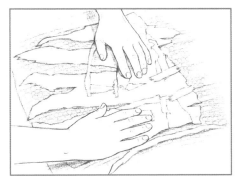

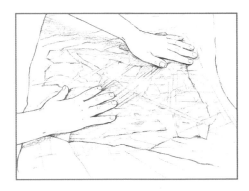

1 First, make the pre-felts. They can be plain, perhaps in contrasting colors, or very patterned; they can include fibers and fabrics to give a textured surface (see page 18); or they can be embellished with stitching. Cut the pre-felts to the desired shape and size.

2 On a piece of thin plastic sheeting, set out the pre-felts with their edges butted together or overlapping, making up the mosaic.

3 Wet the pieces with hot, soapy water and gently ease their edges together, then cover with a second piece of plastic sheeting and press down hard, especially on the edges.

4 Turn the whole piece over. Remove the plastic and inspect the back of the mosaic: you may now need to add a few strands of wool to the back to reinforce the cut edges and make the felt stronger.

5 Replace the plastic and complete the felting process (Stages 3, 4, and 5 of basic felting, pages 11–14).

Adding fabrics and other fibers to felt

There are no precise rules for adding fabrics and fibers to felt. If it works, it works. In general, fabrics made of natural fibers such as silk, cotton, and rayon/viscose are easier to work with and produce a more successful result. (However, with a little hard work and perseverance, some very interesting effects can be achieved with synthetics.)

Added fabrics and fibers need to be anchored to the felt. Those with an open weave are likely to felt in easily, but other types will require wool fibers to be placed over them to improve their chances of felting in. Remember: a piece of fabric that is laid down flat will crinkle and distort as the wool shrinks. Refer to the instructions for basic felting on pages 8–14.

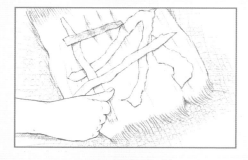

1 Lay out the wool then arrange the fabrics and fibers on top of the wool.

2 Add thin strands of wool to anchor in the fabrics.

3 Cover with net and wet out (see Stage 2 of basic felting, page 10), then continue through Stages 3, 4, and 5, pages 11–14.

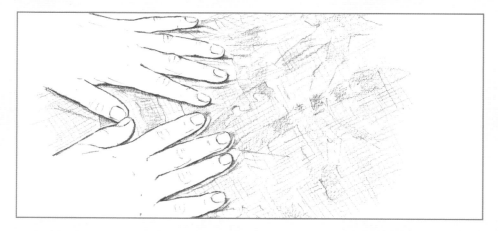

Cobweb felt

Cobweb felt is very soft and fine and, as its name suggests,
gossamer thin and without formal structure. To make it,
follow the procedure for basic felting on pages 8–14.

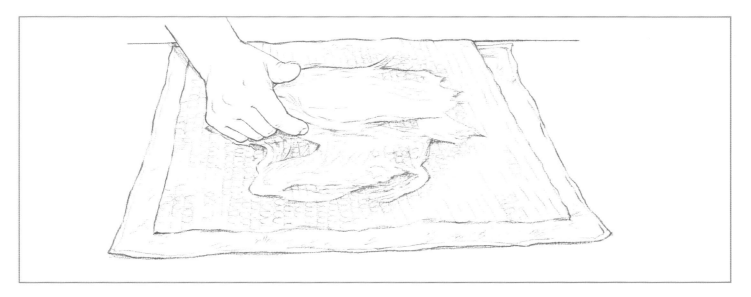

1 Lay out the wool as thinly as you
can, keeping all the fibers running in
the same direction. In general, one
layer of wool will be sufficient;
however, placing a few strands to run
diagonally, or at right angles to the
first layer, will add strength and help
hold the felt together. At this point,
silk fibers, threads, or yarns could
also be added: be experimental.

Proceed to Step 5, Stage 1 of the
basic felting instructions (page 9), then
work through the remaining stages
to complete the felting process. Some
holes may appear in the finished piece,
but this will add to its charm.

Network felt

Network felt is also known as felt lace. It is felt that features a network of holes. The felt is formed by leaving spaces between the tufts of wool as you lay them out, rather than creating a solid rectangle. The wool can be laid as a grid of straight lines (like a lattice), interlocking circles, or a combination of both.

Tip **Add thick woollen yarns to the wool in the grid for extra interest; or place strands across the holes to produce a sub-network of a finer, more delicate character.**

1 Follow the instructions for basic felting on pages 8–14 but in Step 2 of Stage 1, set out the wool in a network. Place the wool for the first layer, in any color and direction you choose, then drape the wool for the second layer over the top, again in any color and direction you choose. The rows may be evenly spaced or could be distributed in order to provide holes of varying sizes.

Move to Step 5, Stage 1 of the instructions for basic felting (page 9) and continue to the end of the process. It is also possible to make network felt by cutting holes in pre-felt and finishing in the usual way.

Cords

Felt cords are fun to make and can have many different uses, from shoelaces to necklaces, bag handles and embellishments.

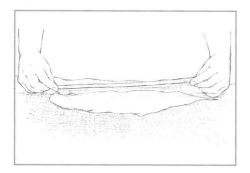

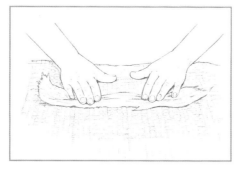

Tip Make a thick cord and use different colored wool for the layers. When it is dry, chop off slices to use for jewellery or buttons.

1 Take a length of merino wool top (dry) and rub it between the palms of your hands to form a long, thin sausage shape. Wet it in hot, soapy water and roll it again on the worksurface.

2 Keep wetting and rolling the sausage until it is the length and thickness that you want, flattening more lengths of wool for further layers and rolling the cord in these.

3 Pour hot, soapy water on the cord and continue rolling until it is very hard. Rinse and leave to dry.

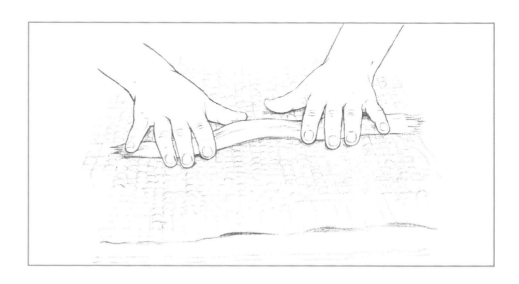

Spikes

Felt spikes are used to embellish items such as bags or hats. They have a point at one end and a root at the other to enable you to attach them.

Make a spike in the same way as a felt cord, but keep one end of the wool dry to use as the root, which you will be able to felt into a base piece of pre-felt.

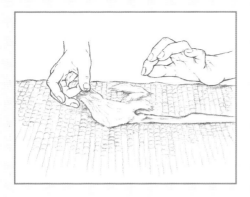

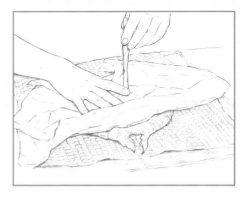

1 Make the spikes by following the instructions for Cords (page 21), and making them shorter. Keep the root end of the spike dry, and form the other end into a point.

2 Make the pre-felt for the base, which the spikes will be attached to, by working to the end of Step 8 in Stage 2 of the basic felting process (page 10).

To attach a spike, spread out the root in a circle and sit the spike on the pre-felt. Anchor in the root by placing strands of wool over it in different directions.

3 Continue to Stage 3, but when you put the thin plastic sheeting on top of the pre-felt, make a hole in the plastic and pull the spike through. This will prevent the spike from being felted down flat as you continue. Wet the plastic a little to make it slippery. Begin rubbing the wool with your hands, in a circular motion, to lock the fibers together. Work around the base of the spike, leaving it standing up. The felting process may take about ten minutes or longer. Roll the spike between your hands to confirm its shape. When all the spikes are firmly felted in, move on to Stages 4 and 5 (pages 12–14), where the whole piece is rolled, shrunk, and finished.

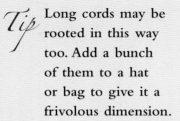

Tip Long cords may be rooted in this way too. Add a bunch of them to a hat or bag to give it a frivolous dimension.

Bobbles

Bobbles make jaunty decorations for hats, bags, and slippers. They can be threaded together to form a necklace. They are ideal for buttons or earrings, either as globes or sliced in half, especially if made up of layers of different colors. Bobbles may also be embellished with beads. Tiny bobbles could be made into stamens for a flower corsage.

1 To make a bobble, take a pinch of wool top (dry) and roll it in a circular motion in the palms of your hands.

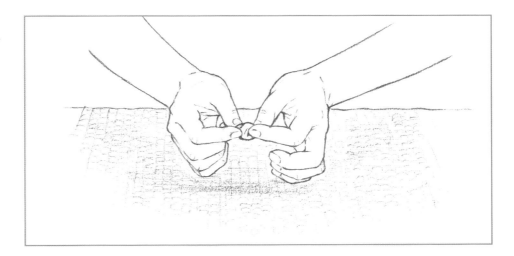

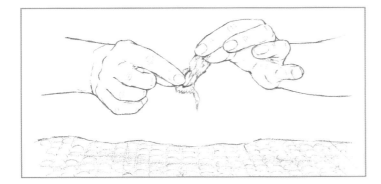

2 Wet it in hot, soapy water and roll it again, then add another layer of wool.

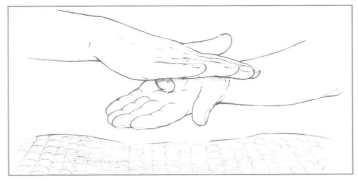

3 Continue wetting, rolling, and adding wool until the bobble is the size you require.
Rinse and leave to dry.

Creating a felt shape

To make a three-dimensional item in felt, you could simply stitch pieces of flat felt together. However, you may need to make a piece of felt in a particular shape. To do this, the felt is worked on a template. Felt can also be shaped over a mold, such as a ball.

Making a free-standing shape

Here is how to create a basic bag or purse shape, joined seamlessly on three sides and open across the top, with a template. The template also acts as a resist — it prevents one side of the shape from felting into the other. The finished item can be further shaped, or blocked, to turn it into a cylindrical container (see page 30).

STAGE 1. MAKING THE TEMPLATE

1 To make a template for a small purse, work out the size and shape you want the finished item to be. Remember that the felt will shrink, so you need to add an allowance around the edge of approximately 25–30 percent.

2 Draw this shape onto plastic foam flooring underlay (obtainable from DIY stores), a piece of pliable plastic, or bubble wrap, and cut out the template.

Tip Templates made from plastic foam underlay produce the best results because they have an edge to work the wool against and so prevent the felt from having ridges around the edges.

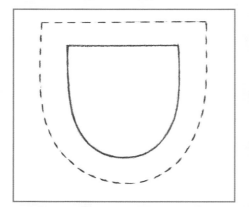

STAGE 2. LAYING OUT THE WOOL

3 Spread an old towel on the work surface and put a piece of bubble wrap on top, with the bubbles facing upwards.

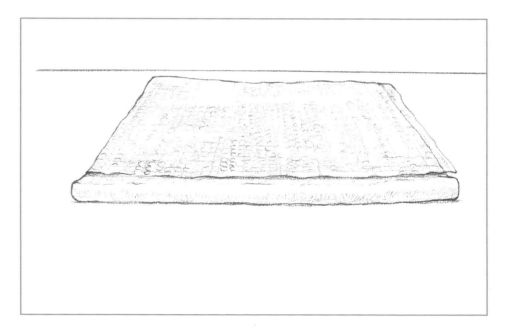

4 Place the template on top of the bubble wrap. Lay pieces of wool horizontally across the template, overlapping the edges of the template by approximately ¾ in (2 cm). Lay a second layer at right angles to the first one, but this time don't lay the wool all the way to the edge of the template to prevent the edges from becoming too thick. Make sure you spread the wool carefully and evenly.

Make between two and six layers, depending on the item. (This small purse would require two layers, a hat three, and a strong bag six.)

STAGE 3. SEALING IN THE TEMPLATE

 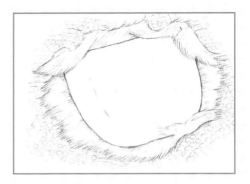 

5 Cover with a piece of net curtain. Sprinkle hot, soapy water over the center of the shape and wet it out (see page 10), but keep the wool that overlaps the edges of the template dry.

6 Remove the net and place a piece of thin plastic sheeting over the work. Using the flat of your hand, press down to spread the water over the template, again keeping the edges dry.

7 Put one hand under the template and the other hand on top, and carefully flip the whole piece over. The template will now be on the top.

8 Slightly wet the edges of the template and then, using the plastic sheeting, gently pull the wool around the edges over the template, feeling the shape of the template as you do so, and press down with the plastic.

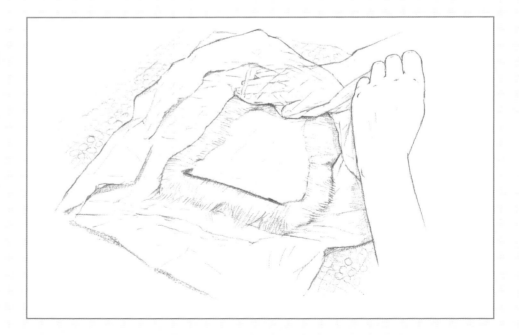

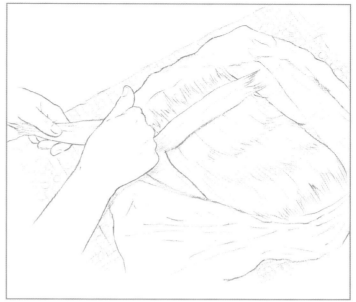

9 Now cover this side of the template with wool. Lay wool horizontally across this second side, overlapping the edges of the template, as in Step 4 above (page 25).

10 Follow this with a vertical layer.

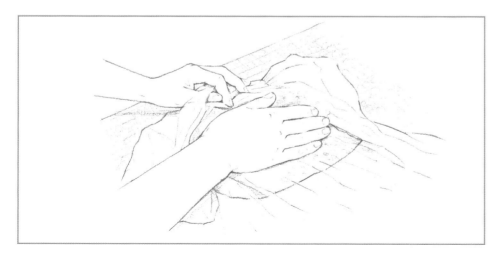

11 Repeat Steps 5 and 6, but there is no need to keep the edges dry at this stage. Flip over again to the first side, folding the excess wool over the edges of the template as before. The template is now totally enclosed.

28

STAGE 4. DECORATING

12 If you wish, you can add decoration to the felt, on one side or both. Add tufts of wool in different colors, or draw shapes or patterns with wool.

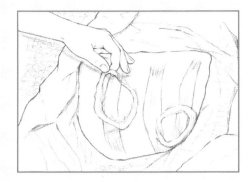

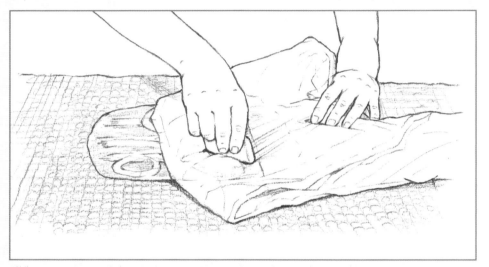

13 Ensure that the wool is completely wet and then cover it with plastic sheeting. If the water does not penetrate the fibers easily, add more soap to help it do so. Do this by carefully lifting the plastic and rubbing soap onto it, then replace it to transfer the soap to the wool.

STAGE 5. FELTING

14 Now felt the wool – see Stage 3 of the basic felting process, page 11.

Note: A fullness may begin to appear in the middle of the shape, but ignore this and continue to work the sides, top, and bottom. When you turn the project over and work the other side, the fullness will disappear. Continue working the edges, gradually moving further towards the center of the shape, turning it frequently, until the fullness at the sides has shrunk away, and the felt fits the template closely. With the plastic still on top, rub the felt all over with the flat of your hand. Do the pinch test (see Step 11, Stage 3 of basic felting, page 11).

Tip If the size of the finished item is crucial, as for a hat, make a sample first in the chosen fibers to ascertain exactly how much it is going to shrink.

STAGE 6. SHRINKING

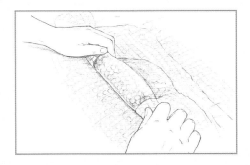

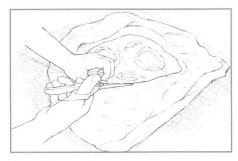

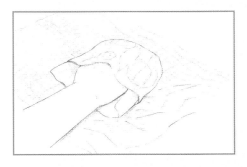

15 Roll up the felt in the bubble wrap. It can be rolled around a piece of dowelling or a rolling pin. Now roll it on the worksurface – from top to bottom and from side to side, until the template inside begins to distort.

16 Remove the felt, insert the point of a sharp pair of scissors into the corner of the top edge of the shape, and cut the top edge open. Leave the template inside.

17 Work the cut edges with hot water and soap, rubbing in all directions. Put your hand inside the shape and rub the felt on the bubble wrap or on a washboard.

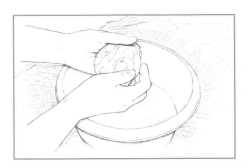

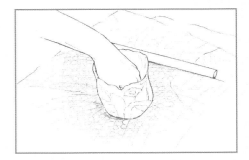

18 Fill a plastic bowl with hot water. With the template still inside the felt shape, immerse the felt. Squeeze out the water, stretch, and reshape it.

19 Roll up the bubble wrap and the felt as one to form a tight bundle. Roll this on the towel. When the felt has shrunk by approximately 30 percent and is no longer stretchy, remove the template from inside. Rinse the felt in cold water.

20 Roll the felt in a towel to remove excess moisture. Pull it back into the desired shape, cover with a cloth and press with an iron. The bag shape is now complete.

Making a cover for a cylindrical container

A basic felt bag shape can be molded into a cylindrical shape and used as a decorative cover. Make a vase by putting a jar inside the cover, use it as an ornamental jacket for a plant holder, or insert a plastic cup inside to make an attractive container for pens and pencils.

MAKING THE TEMPLATE

1 Put a tape measure around the container that is to be covered and measure its circumference to give 'c'. Work out the height the finished cover needs to be to give 'h'.

To allow for the shrinkage of the felt during the making process, the template has to be made bigger than the size of the finished item. Divide the circumference by two and add half as much again to give the measurement 'a'. Add half as much again to the height of the container to give measurement 'b'.

2 Draw a rectangle on a piece of paper: the base and top are measurement 'a' and the sides are measurement 'b'. Round off the two bottom corners of the rectangle (see diagram, right), making sure that the shape is symmetrical by folding the paper in half and cutting the two rounded corners together. This makes the cover easier to block (shape) because there isn't an excess of felt to get rid of.

3 Place the template on plastic foam flooring underlay, trace around it, and cut it out. Follow Steps 1–20 of creating a felt shape (pages 24–29).

4 After shrinking, block the wet shape by inserting the jar or other container into it, and then use hot water and soap to work away any fullness and make the felt fit the jar. Rinse, squeeze to get rid of excess water, then re-block and leave to dry.

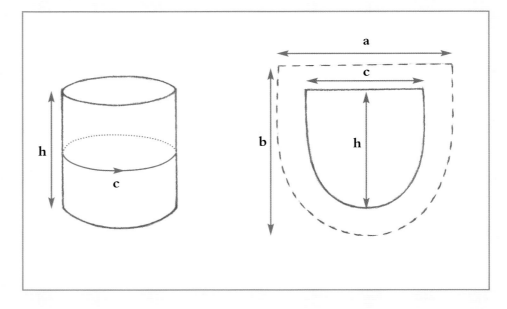

Using a resist

It is useful to be able to make flaps, tucks, or pockets in a piece of felt. To do this, use a resist – a piece of thin plastic cut in the shape of the flap. The resist needs to be bigger on all sides than the flap, except for the hinge edge, which joins the main piece of felt. This is necessary to give space to achieve the dimensions of the flap without joining it to the base layer by mistake.

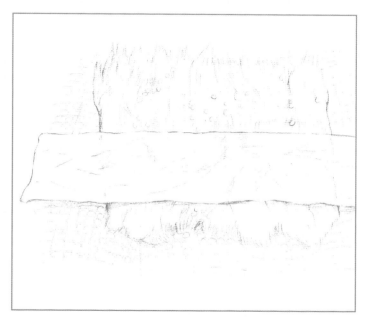

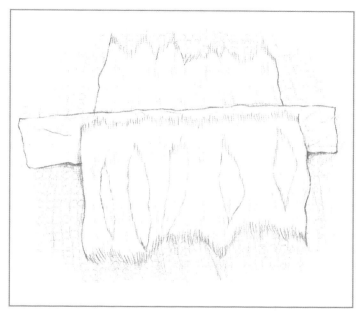

1 After laying out a base layer of wool and wetting it, according to Stages 1 and 2 of the basic felting process (pages 8–10), place the resist on top.

2 Add more wool fibers, covering the resist and running over the base layer, too, at what will be the hinge of the flap (bottom of illustration). The wool should not overhang the other edges of the flap. The resist will prevent the flap layer of wool from felting into the base layer, except at the hinge. Cover the whole thing with a piece of thin plastic sheeting and complete the rest of the felting process through Stages 3, 4 and 5 (pages 11–14).

red

and orange

Shiny berries; fluttering poppies; flaking rust; a soft carpet of autumnal leaves.

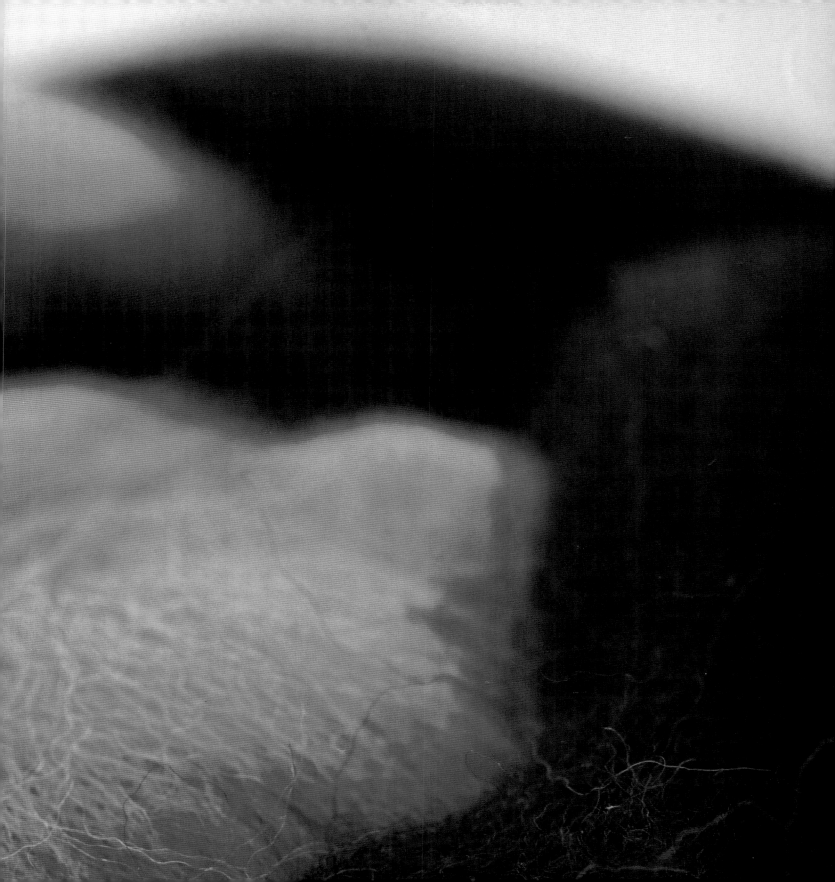

berries

This is a good first project: the shapes are simple but the design allows you to enjoy playing with a selection of rich colors right away. The addition of a small amount of green injects a note of contrast, and wispy silk fibers provide highlights.

Materials

1 oz (30 g) cherry red merino wool top
Tiny quantity each of orange, scarlet, burgundy, terracotta, and green merino wool tops
A few silk fibers

Method

1 Refer to the instructions for basic feltmaking on pages 8–14. Lay out two layers of the cherry red wool in a rectangle, following Stage 1.
2 Tease out small amounts of wool from the other wool tops to make a pattern of spots and circles. Keep the wool fine so that it will adhere to the base felt easily.
3 Scatter the silk fibers lightly over the surface.
4 Cover with net, wet out, and continue the basic feltmaking process through Stages 3, 4 and 5.

Glowing oranges and reds suggest berry-studded hedgerows; wisps of silk evoke autumnal mists.

poppy

Poppies are delicate, like fine silk, but their hairy stems are a complete contrast. This piece echoes that relationship by incorporating silk fabric, trapped by fibers of wool, which crumples when the wool felts. Velvet and chiffon have been added, too, for an extra-sumptuous texture. 'Poppy' is ideal for making a cushion cover; use a piece of velvet for the other side.

Materials

1½ oz (40 g) dark red merino wool top
1½ oz (40 g) poppy red merino wool top
1 yd x 2 in (90 x 5 cm) ruby red silk fabric
Two strips, 1 yd x ⅜ in (90 x 1 cm) dark red or burgundy silk velvet
8 x 4 in (20 x 10 cm) pink chiffon in rayon or silk
A few pink and orange silk fibers

Method

1 Refer to the instructions for basic feltmaking on pages 8–14, and for adding fabrics and other fibers to felt on page 18.
2 Using the dark red around the edges and the poppy red in the center, lay out three layers of wool in a rectangle.
3 Cut the ruby red silk as follows: four strips, 29½ x ⅜ in (75 x 1 cm); one piece, 6 x 2 in (15 x 5 cm).
4 Place the small rectangle of ruby silk in the center of the wool, and arrange the strips of silk and velvet around it. Cut the chiffon into four pieces and set them out around the central piece of ruby silk.
5 Add the silk fibers, then cover the design with a very fine layer of wisps of wool to trap the fabrics in the wool.
6 Cover with net and wet out.
7 When thoroughly wet, replace the net with plastic sheeting and continue the basic feltmaking process through Stages 3, 4 and 5.

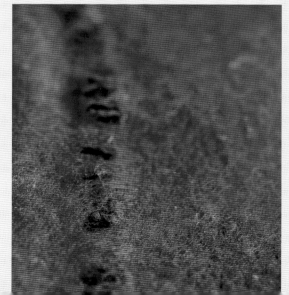

This piece melds strong color and delicate fabrics: the essence of a poppy.

rust

Rust can be beautiful – its colors range from deep red, burgundy, and orange to purple and blue. It has wonderful textures, too: as iron corrodes layers peel off, leaving crusty, flaking edges. Use the resist technique to emulate these layers and build up a rusty-looking surface.

Materials
½ oz (15 g) in total of burgundy, wine, rust, orange, and cherry red merino wool tops

¼ oz (5 g) Wensleydale wool in a graduated dye from orange/rust through to purple/grey-blue

8 x 6 in (20 x 15 cm) rust silk fabric, cut into rough strips

10 x ¾ in (25 x 2 cm) red douppion silk fabric, cut into scraps with uneven edges

16 x 2⅜ in (40 x 6 cm) magenta chiffon, cut into two strips

⅛ oz (3 g) purple or grey-blue silk fibers

Additional equipment
Two pieces, 4 x 8 in (10 x 20 cm) plastic (for resist)

Method
1 Refer to the instructions for basic feltmaking on pages 8–14, and for adding fabrics and other fibers to felt on page 18.

2 Lay down two layers of wool tops using some of each of the colors.

3 In the center of the wool rectangle, put some of the most vibrant orange/rust Wensleydale wool and some strips of the silk and chiffon.

4 Wet out.

5 Refer to the instructions for using a resist on page 31. Place the plastic resists in a cross shape at the center.

6 Lay the remainder of the wool, fabrics, and fibers vertically over the surface, leaving a few gaps over the resists in places, and ensuring that the fabrics are anchored in with wisps of wool.

7 Cover with net and finish the basic feltmaking process through Stages 3, 4 and 5.

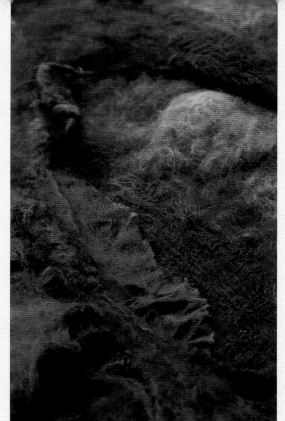

Chunky textures, curly fleece, and layering interpret the appearance of rusting metal.

forest floor

The appliqué method is used for this project. Some of the most striking appliqué designs are created by using pre-felts in strongly contrasting textures and patterns. The addition of embroidery, either by hand or by machine, would further enhance this piece of felt.

Materials
⁵⁄₁₆ oz (8 g) spring green merino wool top
⁵⁄₁₆ oz (8 g) red merino wool top
Tiny quantity black merino wool top
³⁄₈ oz (10 g) orange merino wool top

Method
1 Refer to the instructions for basic feltmaking on pages 8–14, and for making pre-felt on page 16.
2 Lay out a layer of green wool. Cover this with a fine layer of red wool, placing the fibers at right angles to those in the first layer. Put a few wisps of black wool on top. Follow the instructions to the end of Stage 3, completing the base pre-felt.
3 Make an orange pre-felt that is a little smaller than the base pre-felt: lay out the orange wool, add a few wisps of black, and pre-felt.
4 Cut through the orange pre-felt diagonally, from a bottom corner, in varying wavy lines. Cut to the top of the felt but do not cut right through the edge. Make about five cuts.
5 Refer to the instructions for appliqué on page 16. Place the orange pre-felt on top of the base pre-felt and spread it out so that the base felt is exposed.
6 Add a few more black wisps and some green ones, and then complete the basic feltmaking process through Stages 4 and 5.

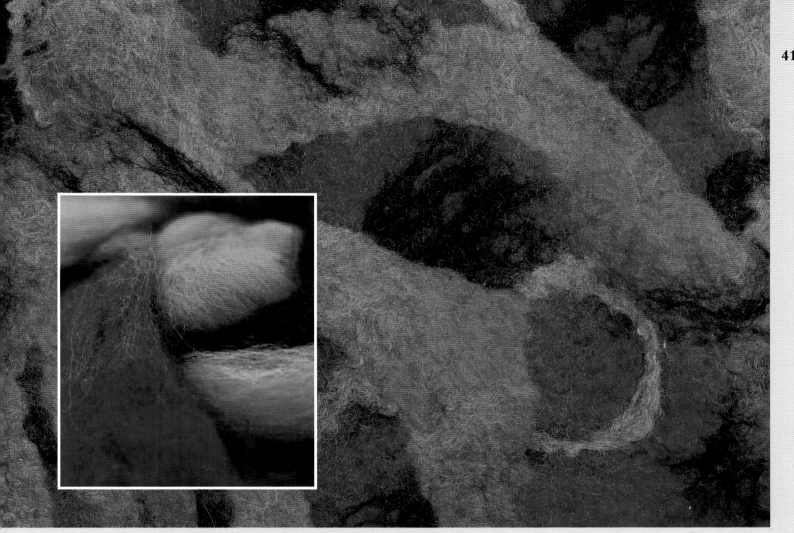

Nature weaves her own carpet for the forest floor: a tapestry of red, orange, and green.

yellow

Golden honeycomb; strange, stripy gourds; proud, canary-yellow sunflowers.

honeycomb

This project shows you how to create a cell-like structure, which is great fun to make. Marbles have been used here to do this, but other objects such as buttons, coins, pebbles, or even flat pieces of plastic could be used instead: they all act as a resist.

The marbles may be removed after felting, or left inside. Depending on the effect you want, the marbles can be cut out from the front or the back of the felt. Cut a hole in both if you like, or alternate between the two. You may like to insert little felt balls into the holes.

Materials

1¾ oz (50 g) yellow merino wool top

Method

1 Refer to the instructions for basic feltmaking on pages 8–14. Lay out two layers of wool.

2 Place the marbles on this base and cover with two more layers of wool. The technique works best if there is some space between the marbles so that the cells remain separated.

3 Cover with net and wet out, ensuring that the wool between the marbles is wet and flat, too.

4 Replace the net with plastic sheeting and move on to Stage 3, felting. Rub the felt in and around the marbles, keeping it wet and soapy.

5 Complete Stage 4, shrinking. It can be difficult to roll the felt because it has such a lumpy texture, and this is where a washboard can be very useful for applying friction.

6 Dry the completed felt thoroughly before cutting it to remove the marbles. Reshape the cells with your fingers.

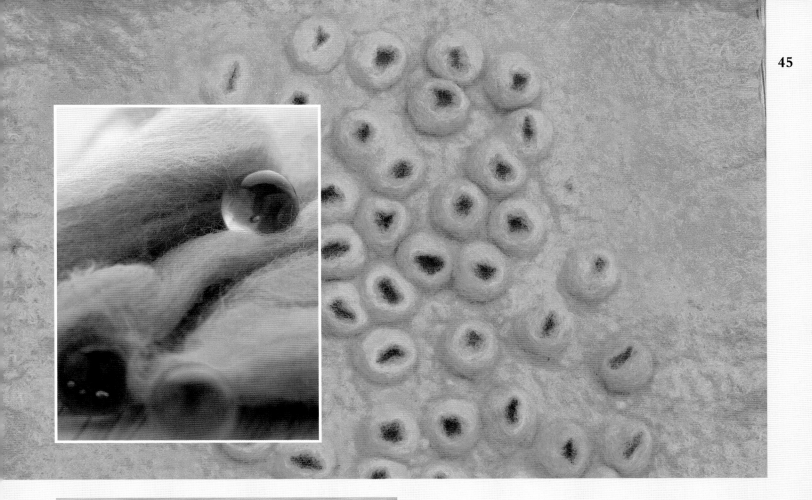

Honeycomb's intricate network of interlocking cells is echoed in the nubbly texture of this felt.

gourd

Ornamental gourds grow in strange, knobby shapes. To recreate this effect, the felt is tied around a pole, over a string of large beads, and then left to dry. This causes the felt to distort and stretch, so that when the string is removed, the felt has an amazing undulating texture. Beads are then sewn into the grooves for further embellishment.

Materials
⅞ oz (25 g) yellow ochre merino wool top
Tiny quantity orange merino wool top
Tiny quantity green merino wool top
A few strands green silk thread
Amber beads and thread to match

Additional equipment
Large beads loosely threaded on a long length of string
2¼ yd (2 m) string
12 in (30 cm) wooden dowelling or plastic pipe
1–2 in (2.5–5 cm) in diameter

Method
1 Refer to the instructions for basic feltmaking on pages 8–14. Lay out two layers of the yellow ochre wool.
2 Add orange stripes, about 2 in (5 cm) apart. Sprinkle on the strands of green wool and the silk threads.
3 Wet out and complete the feltmaking process to the end of Stage 5, making sure that the felt is well shrunk.
4 Take the string of beads and secure it to one end of the dowelling.
5 Secure the corner of the felt (with string) over the bead string on the dowelling. Wrap the felt around the dowelling, pulling the string tightly around it and trapping the beads underneath. Wrap the string around the dowelling about fifteen times, spacing the spirals about ⅜ in (1 cm) apart.
6 Push the felt together so that it bunches up, and tie the string to the dowelling.
7 Leave the felt to dry and then remove it from the dowelling.
8 Sew the amber beads randomly across the felt.

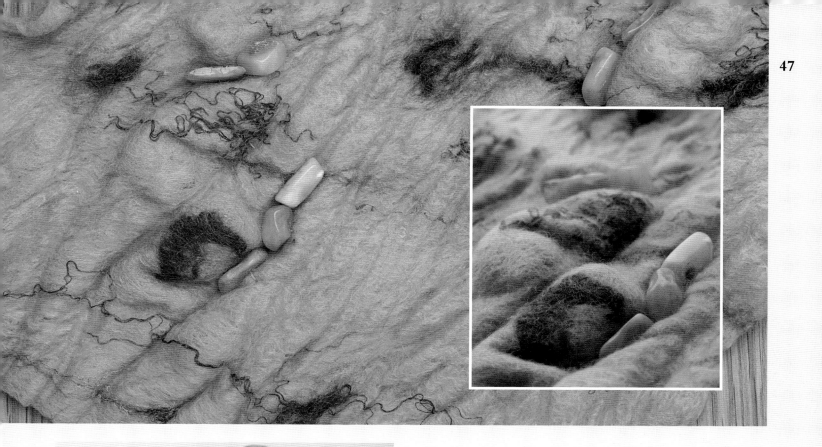

Explore a gourd's combination of color, pattern, shape, and texture to create a stunning visual effect.

sunflower

In the height of summer, fields of sunflowers are a cheerful sight. Their strong yellows, russet reds and browns are inspirational, and the sunflower motif is perfect for textile design. The felt in this project is shaped to resemble the flower. You can use the finished item to make a summery bag or a striking cushion.

Materials

1½ oz (40 g) strong yellow merino wool top
Handful yellow-orange curly Wensleydale wool
Tiny quantity green merino wool top
3⅛ in (8 cm) diameter circle dark red-brown velvet
Rayon machine embroidery thread in yellow, gold, and brown

Method

1 Refer to the instructions for basic feltmaking on pages 8–14, and for adding fabrics and fibers to felt on page 18.
2 Lay out two layers of yellow merino wool in a circle.
3 Create a second circle, the same size as the first, on a separate part of the bubble wrap. Add an inner circle of Wensleydale wool, with the pieces of wool laid to point towards the edge.
4 Create a third circle out of green wool, again in a separate area. Make it a third the size of the first two. Place the circle of velvet in the center and cover it thinly with fibers of green wool.
5 Complete the feltmaking process on all three circles, working through Stages 2, 3, 4 and 5, but do not dry the felt.
6 Cut the edge of each circle into petal shapes. Work on the cut edges with soap and water, sealing them by rubbing them against the bubble wrap.
7 Rinse each circle, squeeze to remove excess water, and press it with a warm iron. Stretch each shape and reshape the petals. Leave to dry.
8 Arrange the three petal circles on top of each other, with the plain one at the bottom, the one containing Wensleydale wool over it, and the green one on top.
9 Recreate the seeds in the center of a sunflower on the green petals, using machine embroidery in tiny, circular movements, and stitching through all three of the petal circles to fix them together.

The hot colors and bold shape of these imposing flowers can be enjoyed all year round in felt.

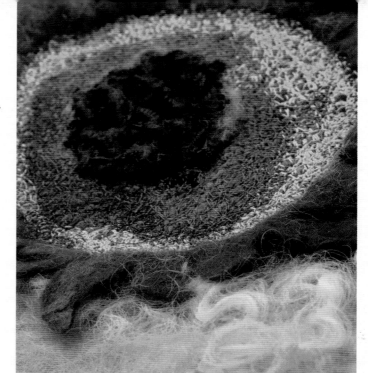

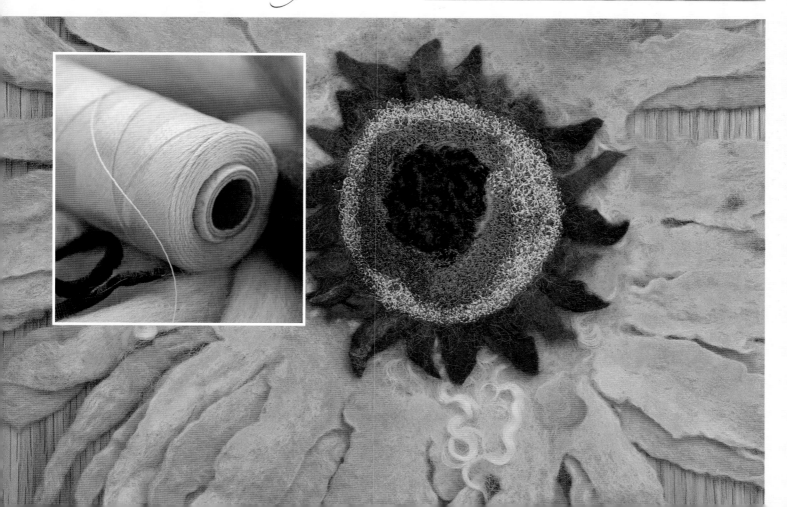

green

Primeval ferns; dense, cushiony moss;
a patchwork of cottage garden greens.

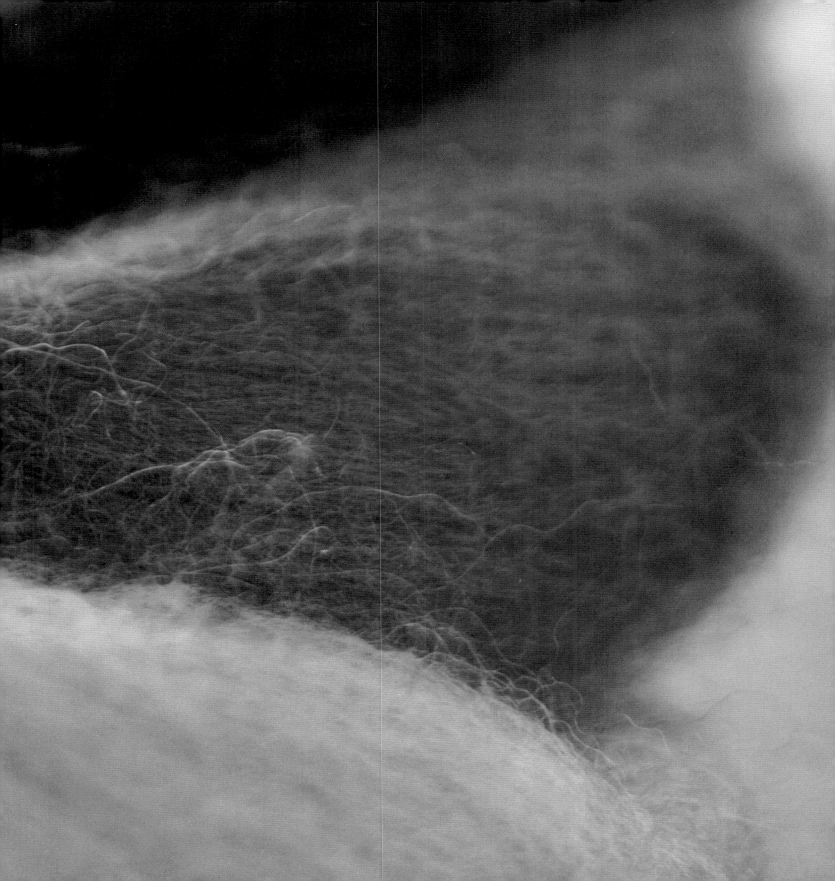

fern

The feathery shapes of intermingled ferns create an ethereal pattern. This project features the appliqué technique: fern shapes are appliquéd to an olive green background. If you want to put a little more work in, you can even make the fronds stand away from the felt – see Step 6 of the Method.

Materials

¾ oz (20 g) olive merino wool top (background)
⅜ oz (10 g) each of 2–3 shades green merino wool top (ferns)
6 x 4 in (5 x 10 cm) dress net (in a light green shade)
A few silk fibers in greens and gold

Method

1 Refer to the instructions for basic feltmaking on pages 8–14, for making pre-felt and appliquéd felt on page 16, and for adding fabrics and fibers to felt on page 18.

2 For the ferns, make three pre-felts from each of the three greens. Lay out the wool in two fine layers, with a few silk fibers on top. Allow to dry.

3 Cut out a selection of ferns in different sizes. Make cardboard templates to help you to do this if you wish. Cut ferns from the dress net, too.

4 Make an olive green pre-felt for the background, using two layers of wool. Leave wet.

5 Arrange the ferns on the wet base, then complete the felting process, working through Stages 4 and 5 of basic feltmaking.

6 (Optional.) You could build up layers of ferns to give a slightly three-dimensional effect. After placing the first layer of ferns, use a thin strip of plastic to act as a resist on additional ferns, so that they remain slightly proud along one edge instead of felting into the background. (See using a resist on page 31.)

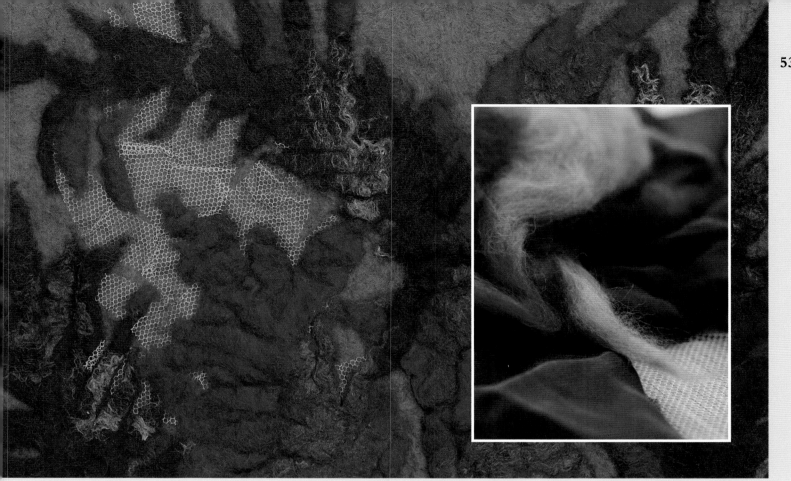

Delicate shapes in a
symphony of greens:
a cool forest glade.

moss

The surface of moss makes velvet an obvious choice for giving this piece a subtle sheen and texture. Swatches of velvet, together with strips of silk, are felted onto a base of muted greens. When the felt shrinks, the fabrics ruche, providing an intriguing and tactile extra dimension.

Materials

1–1½ oz (30–40 g) in total of merino wool tops in three shades of green (dark, medium, and light)
12 x 12 in (30 x 30 cm) green velvet
4 strips gold velvet, each 18 x ¾ in (46 x 2 cm)
8 x 8 in (20 x 20 cm) green silk fabric

Method

1 Refer to the instructions for basic feltmaking on pages 8–14, and for adding fabrics and fibers to felt on page 18.

2 Lay out a layer of wool in the darkest of the three greens.

3 Place a second layer of medium green wool on top. The fibers should be at right angles to those in the first layer.

4 Cut the velvet and silk into pieces and lay them on top of the wool in the required design.

5 Use wisps of the lightest green wool to trap the fabrics into the felt.

6 Cover with net and complete Stages 2, 3, 4, and 5 of basic feltmaking.

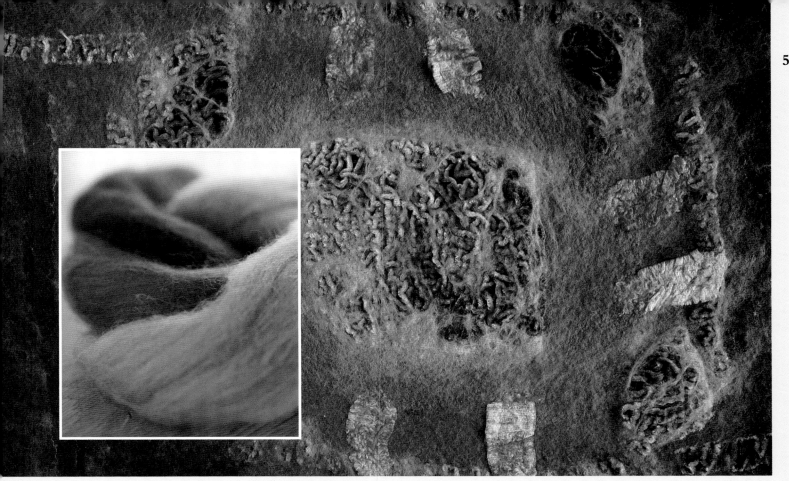

A rich green base patterned with vibrant colors and textures evokes the beauty of moss on stone.

cottage garden

Create the delight of a cottage garden in its jumble of color, shape, and form. In this project, tiny scraps of vibrant silk and velvet have been used to lift the underlying network of dark greens and purples. By adding a few seeding stitches, the velvet is made to ruche in a very organic way, distorting the stitched threads, when the felt is shrunk. The mosaic technique is used in this project.

Materials

⅜–½ oz (10–15 g) in total of blended merino wool tops in a selection of greens and ochre

⅜–½ oz (10–15 g) in total of blended merino wool tops in purple, navy, and burgundy

2⅜ x ¾ in (6 x 2 cm) orange silk fabric

2⅜ x ¾ in (6 x 2 cm) lime green velvet

6 x 1½ in (15 x 4 cm) purple/pink rayon georgette

6 x 1½ in (15 x 4 cm) green rayon georgette

A few gold silk fibers

Stranded embroidery cotton in pink, burgundy, green, and orange

Method

1 Refer to the instructions for basic feltmaking on pages 8–14, and for making pre-felt on page 16. Make two pre-felts: one from each set of the blended colors.

2 Refer to the instructions for making a mosaic on page 16. Cut shapes from the pre-felts and arrange them as you wish.

3 Refer to the instructions for adding fabrics and fibers to felt on page 18. Position the silk, velvet, and georgette fabrics, and the gold silk fibers, trapping them with a few wool fibers.

4 Wet out and cover with plastic sheeting. Flip the piece over to the reverse, add a few wool fibers where needed, to secure the joins, and turn it over to the front again.

5 Lift the plastic and add some soap to the underside, then replace it on the front of the felt. Begin Stage 3, basic felting, and rub carefully where the pieces join, working on them just enough for them to start felting in. Leave the felt to dry.

6 Now work seed stitch over the pieces of silk, velvet, and georgette. Use other embroidery stitches in various locations across the felt, as the mood takes you.

7 Wet out again and complete Stages 3, 4, and 5 of the basic feltmaking process.

An explosion of color and texture: the charm of a cottage garden is that there are no rules.

blue

Inky rock pools; foaming, blue-green waves; bright blue alpine flowers.

rock pool

A mysterious rock pool, garlanded with seaweed, perhaps with creatures lurking in the depths — created by adding silk fibers and crinkled fabrics to the felt. To give the piece an extra dimension, pleats have been loosely stitched into the reverse. The mosaic technique has been used for this project.

Materials
½ oz (15 g) dark blue merino wool top
½ oz (15 g) green merino wool top
6 x 8 in (15 x 20 cm) dark blue silk fabric
4 x ¾ in (10 x 2 cm) lime green silk fabric
4 x 2 in (10 x 5 cm) burgundy silk velvet
Small quantity gold silk fibers
Tiny quantity white silk fibers
Red/burgundy novelty yarn
Stranded embroidery cotton in light green and red

Method
1 Refer to the instructions for basic feltmaking on pages 8–14, and for making a pre-felt on page 16. You are going to make two pre-felts: one blue and one green.
2 First, lay out two fine layers of blue wool.
3 Refer to the instructions for adding fabrics and fibers to felt on page 18. Cut the blue and green silk into narrow strips. Arrange some of the blue strips and all of the green strips vertically on top of the wool. Overlay the strips with fine wisps of blue wool.
4 Wet out and finish the pre-felt to the end of Stage 3 of basic feltmaking. Leave to dry.
5 Now make the green pre-felt. Lay out two fine layers of the green wool. Incorporate the white and the gold silk fibers. Add the remaining strips of blue silk and secure with fine wisps of green wool.
6 Wet out and finish the pre-felt to the end of Stage 3 of basic feltmaking. Leave to dry.
7 Cut each pre-felt into several pieces. Now arrange the pieces as desired, slightly overlapping them. Refer to the instructions for making a mosaic on page 17, and bond the pieces together. Leave to dry.
8 Cut the velvet into strips. Use it to decorate the felt, stitching it in place.
9 Use the novelty yarn and embroidery cotton to embroider the surface.
10 Complete Stages 4 and 5 of basic feltmaking.
11 If you wish, you can stitch loose pleats into the underside of the piece in order to give it a more three-dimensional shape.

Rock pools are intriguing: what is in their blue-green depths?

wave

This project features network felt, creating a lacy surface. Select as many different shades of blue and purple (and a touch of green) as you can: when intertwined these will produce a graduated look, which is more interesting than a single, plain color. The colors may be blended, by hand or with carders, before using (see page 15). Silk and other fibers are added to the wool; these will distort as the felt shrinks, giving the felt a finely veined appearance with a slight sheen.

Materials

1 oz (30g) in total of merino wool tops in a selection of blues, purples, and greens
Small quantity white or cream silk fibers
Small quantity silk fibers in the same shades as the wool tops

Method

1 Refer to the instructions for basic feltmaking on pages 8–14, and for network felt on page 20. Lay out the wool in a grid pattern, to your design, setting it out in a single layer.
2 Distribute all the other fibers on top.
3 Proceed to Stage 2 of basic feltmaking, covering with net and wetting out. When thoroughly wet and flat, remove the net and replace it with thin plastic sheeting.
4 Start Stage 3, felting, checking that the structure stays as you have positioned it. Reposition if necessary, gently using your finger to push the fibers back into place.
5 Complete Stages 4 and 5.
6 Stretch the piece into shape, cover with a cotton cloth and then press with a moderate iron to smooth it out.

A wave crashes onto a pebbly shore in a froth of foam: capture it in a network of swirling blues.

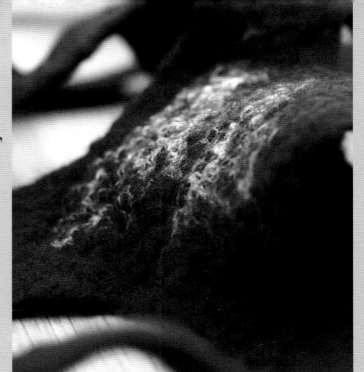

alpine meadow

As a first three-dimensional project, this is a simple one to try. It shows you how to create a basic bag shape, which is joined seamlessly on three sides and open at the top. As long as the wool is layered evenly and the felt is fully shrunk, the bag should be firm enough to hold its shape well.

Materials
1½ oz (40 g) bright blue merino wool top
Tiny quantity purple merino wool top
Tiny quantity white merino wool top
A few silk fibers

Additional equipment
Template of required size (see page 24)

Method
1 Refer to the instructions for creating a felt shape on pages 24–29.
2 Follow the steps, laying out two layers of wool.
3 At Step 13, when the template has been completely enclosed, decorate with strips of purple wool, circles of white wool, and silk fibers.
4 Continue to Step 20. If you want to shape the felt further by blocking it into the shape of a container, refer to the instructions for making a cover for a cylindrical container on page 30.

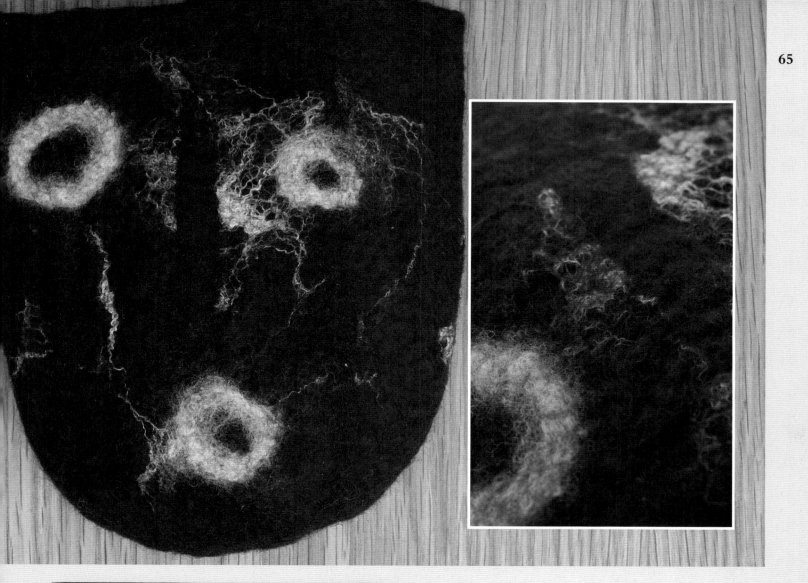

White silk fibers pick out drops of dew on royal-blue alpine blooms.

pink
and purple

A magical coral reef; downy
plums; polished eggplants;
a spiky artichoke.

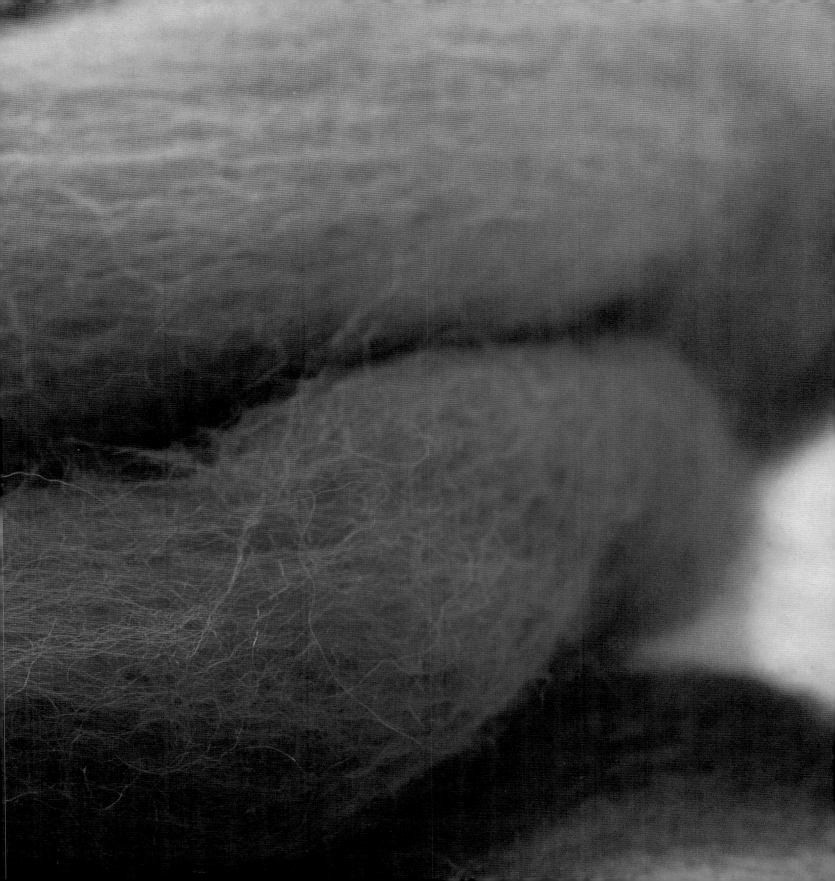

coral

This may look like a fairly complex piece of work, but just follow the instructions for adding fabrics to felt, and for the mosaic technique. The fabrics must be securely anchored to the felt for a successful result. At the pre-felt stage, after cutting and rearranging, a light covering of wool may be added to the surface and the underside to help bond the fabrics to the felt.

Materials

⅜ oz (10 g) white merino wool top
¼ oz (5 g) yellow-green merino wool top
¼ oz (5 g) dark pink merino wool top
Tiny quantity light green merino wool top
12 squares, 3 x 3 in (7.5 x 7.5 cm) scraps of silk
   fabric in pinks and oranges
4 x 4 in (10 x 10 cm) pink dress net
4 in (10 cm) diameter circle blue silk organza
Small piece purple chiffon, cut roughly into a
   flower shape

Method

1 Refer to the instructions for basic feltmaking on pages 8–14, for making pre-felt on page 16, and for adding fabrics and fibers to felt on page 18.
2 Make a piece of pre-felt from white wool, laying half the silk squares symmetrically over the surface, and trapping them with wisps of pink wool.
3 Make a pre-felt with the yellow-green wool, using the remainder of the silk squares and trapping them into place with light green wool.
4 Cut both pre-felts into strips, snipping through the center of the silk squares.
5 Refer to the mosaic technique on page 17. Arrange the strips next to each other, slightly overlapping them and turning some from top to bottom, ensuring that the colors alternate.
6 Cut the net into strips and place it over the joins. Add the silk circle and the chiffon flower.
7 Add a few more wisps of pink wool where needed to trap in fabric edges.
8 Wet out and cover with plastic sheeting, pressing it down over the joins. Carefully turn the piece over and add more wisps of pink wool, horizontally, across the joins. Cover with plastic sheeting. (If you need to add more soap to the felt, apply it to the plastic sheeting before placing it over the felt.)
9 Complete the felt through Stages 3, 4, and 5 of basic feltmaking.

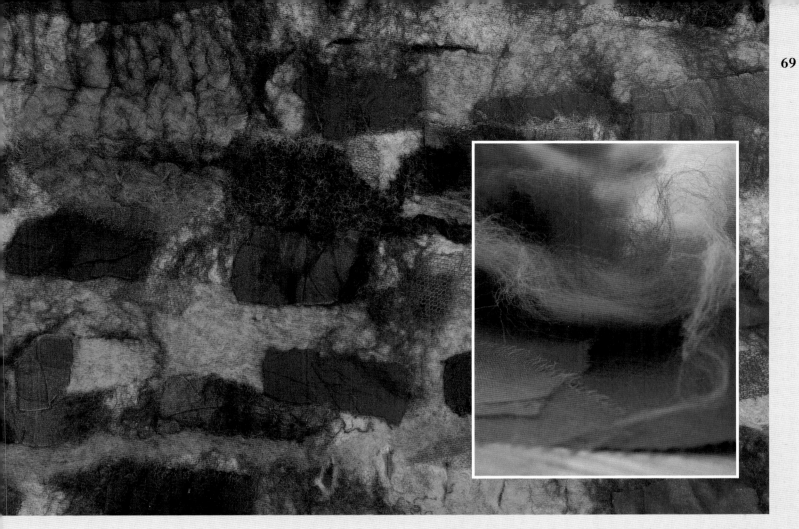

Shapes, textures, and vivid colors blend to create all the fascination of a coral reef.

plum

The cobweb technique used to make this piece means that holes may appear in the felt, and these are an integral part of its overall effect. Cobweb felt has fine draping qualities, and it could be made to a length sufficient for a luxurious scarf or wrap. Remember: if it is to be worn, it is important to fully shrink the felt to ensure that it will wear well and not become pilled or fluffy.

Materials
⅜ oz (10 g) in total of merino wool tops
  in a selection of purples and dark pinks
Tiny quantity deep pink silk fibers

Method
1 Blend the wool colors using carders, if you have them, or by hand (see page 15).
2 Refer to the instructions for basic feltmaking on pages 8–14. Lay out one even layer of wool.
3 Spread the silk fibers across the top and follow the instructions for making cobweb felt on page 19.
4 For a slightly different look, blend the silk fibers in with the wool at the beginning.
5 When completed, press the felt and pull it into shape while it is still damp.

The shiny silk fibers on the matte surface of this felt emulate the bloom on luscious ripe plums.

eggplant

This piece would make a great bag: just use another piece of felt for the back. It could also be turned into a cushion by using fabric for the underside. The surface could be further embellished with stitching, beads, or sequins.

Materials

3⅛ oz (90 g) aubergine merino wool top
6 x 6 in (15 x 15 cm) Devoré velvet in a pink
   and purple colorway
6 x 6 in (15 x 15 cm) purple silk organza
½ yd x ¾ in (50 x 2 cm) deep pink velvet
½ yd x ¾ in (50 x 2 cm) dark purple velvet
½ yd x 2 in (50 x 5 cm) dark orange chiffon
Small quantity white silk fibers
Reel of golden yellow rayon machine
   embroidery thread

Method

1 Refer to the instructions for basic feltmaking on pages 8–14, and for adding fabrics and fibers to felt on page 18.
2 Lay out two even layers of aubergine wool.
3 Arrange the fabrics and silk fibers on top as you wish. Place wisps of wool over them. These will trap them securely when the piece is felted.
4 Cover with net and wet out. Replace the net with plastic sheeting and continue by working through Stages 3, 4 and 5 of basic feltmaking.
5 Allow the felt to dry and embellish with free machine embroidery using the rayon thread.

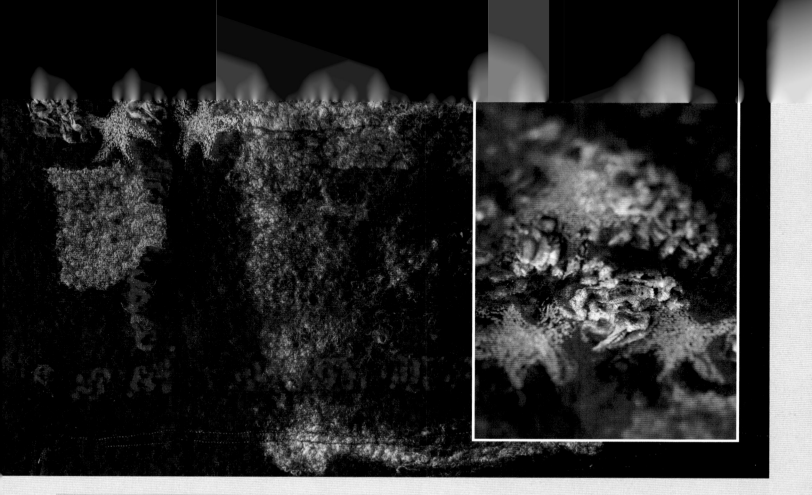

Silk threads mirror the sheen of a glossy eggplant; embroidery is used to suggest the star-shaped cap.

artichoke

The thistle-like globe artichoke is a fascinating plant with leathery petals and a bright pink or purple flower head. To emulate these shapes, plastic resists have been used. This artichoke would make a very attractive purse or bag.

Materials
½ oz (15 g) pink merino wool top
¾ oz (20 g) green merino wool top
Tiny quantity purple silk fibers
Small quantity burgundy wool top

Additional equipment
Plastic (for resist): 1 piece, 7¾ x 9¾ in (20 x 25 cm)

Method
1 Refer to the instructions for basic feltmaking on pages 8–14, and for making pre-felt on page 16. Lay out two layers of the pink wool in an oval shape, and spread the purple silk fibers thinly over the top. Wet out.
2 Refer to the instructions for using a resist on page 31. Lay a strip of plastic across the pink oval to cover most of the upper part, leaving some of the wool exposed for the next layer to adhere to.
3 Lay two layers of green wool, with a little burgundy on top, on the bottom of the pink oval. It should extend upwards on to the plastic, covering almost all of it, and downwards beyond the edge of the pink wool. Wet out.
4 Cover the top half of the green wool with another strip of plastic, leaving the lower part of the green wool uncovered. Wet out.
5 Lay a third and final layer of green wool at the bottom of the artichoke, extending it over the plastic strip.
6 Complete the pre-felt by working Stage 3, felting.
7 Carefully lifting each layer of the green, one row at a time, cut V-shapes into the pre-felt to make the petals. Try to arrange them so that the points of one row fit between the cutouts of the previous row.
8 Complete Stages 4 and 5.
9 If you wish, insert a few stitches in order to make loose pleats in the underside, at the bottom, to make a more rounded shape.

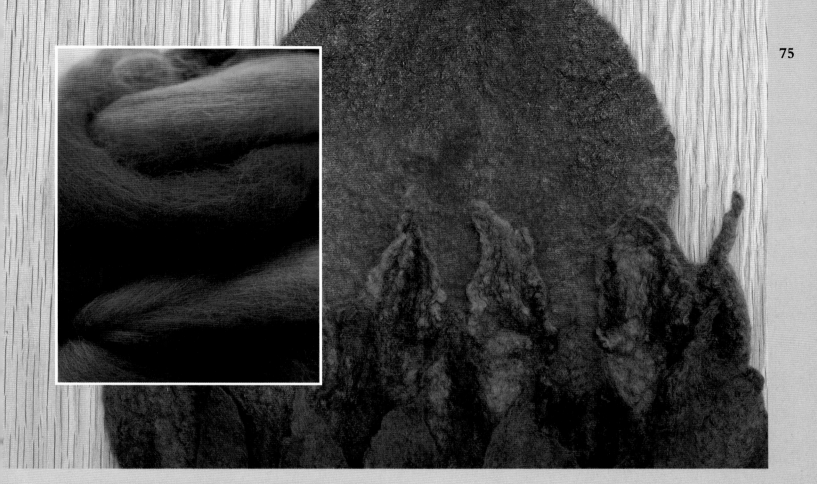

Spiky petals in earthy green shot through with burgundy hug the pink heart of the artichoke.

naturals

Delicately shaped shells; a wiry, spotted fawn; sea-smoothed, patterned pebbles.

shell

This delicate design creates the effect of a drawing of a shell on a piece of felt. Simply by laying a thin strand of dark wool over a pale background, you can see how the fibers shrink together to form irregular lines and patterns. You can experiment further with lustrous embroidery threads to add detail and texture to the shell.

Materials

1 oz (30 g) cream merino wool top
¼ oz (5 g) black merino wool top

Method

1 Make a sketch of the shell design that you want to 'draw' on the felt.
2 Refer to the instructions for basic feltmaking on pages 8–14. Lay out two thin, even layers of cream wool.
3 Cover with net and wet out, as if you were going to felt it. Remove the net carefully.
4 Pull out a long, thin strand of black wool. Following your sketch, put the end of the strip on the cream wool base and hold it with your forefinger. Using your other hand, 'draw' the design on the felt.
5 Replace the net and continue through Stages 3, 4, and 5 to felt and shrink the piece.

Contrasting black and cream inspired by natural treasures from the seashore.

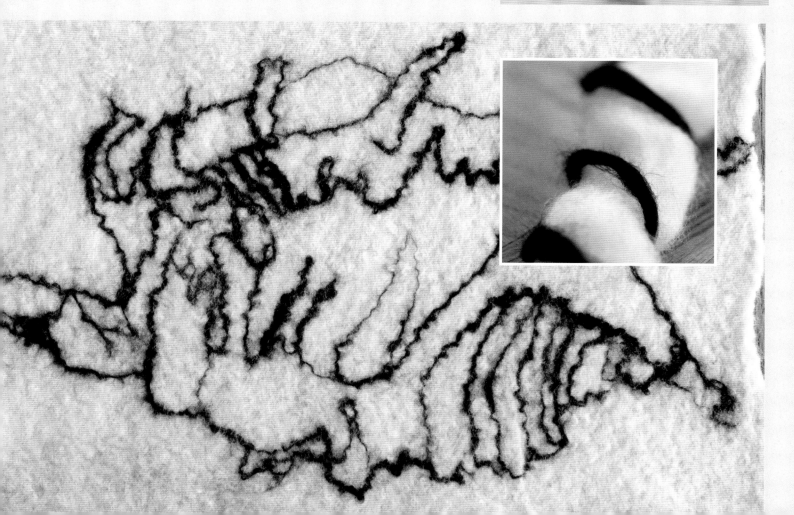

fawn

None of the wools used in this project has been dyed, but all were washed and carded before use. They have a coarser texture than the merino wool used in other projects. All wools have their own peculiarities and should be tested out before being used for a complete project. Some are more difficult to felt than others. Some will felt well; some will be harder-wearing than merino.

Materials
1½ oz (40 g) natural/cream fin wool
⅜ oz (10 g) each of Black Welsh, Jacob, llama and blue-faced Leicester wool
⅛ oz (3 g) burgundy merino wool top
Tiny quantity silk noil
¼ oz (5 g) white/cream silk fibers

Method
1 Refer to the instructions for basic feltmaking on pages 8–14. Lay out a layer of the fin wool.
2 Dividing the surface into five equal parts, leave the center part empty and lay a layer of each of the other four wools in the four remaining parts.
3 Fill the center part with the white silk fibers, allowing them to overlap the wool at either side slightly.
4 Decorate with the silk noil and the burgundy merino wool.
5 Felt in the usual way, working through Stages 2, 3, 4, and 5.

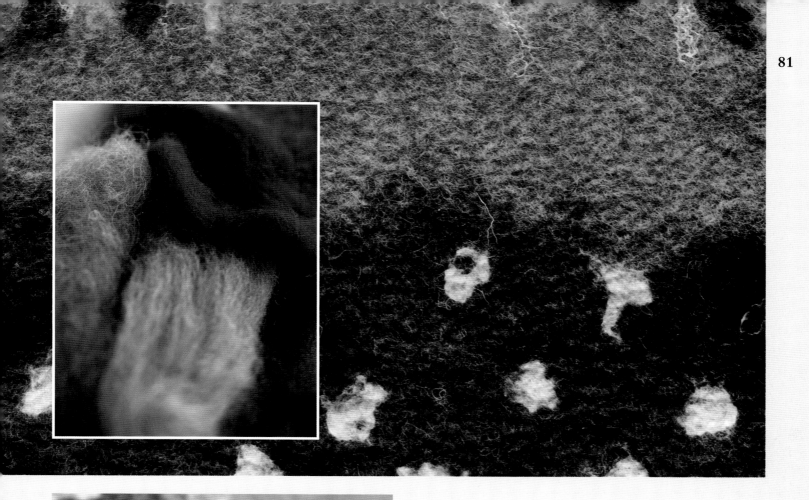

The muted tones of coarse, wiry wools resemble the fur of a young fawn in spring.

pebbles

In this project you can attempt to replicate the veining, markings, and colors of rock in felt that is worked over pebbles used as a base. The pebbles could be used as doorstops or paperweights; you could also make them in vibrant colors.

Materials

⅛ oz (3 g) each of merino wool tops in black, grey, beige, and white
Tiny quantity silk fibers
A selection of smooth stones

Method

1 Refer to the instructions for basic feltmaking on pages 8–14. Wet a pebble with soapy water, wrap a small amount of wool around it and wet it again.
2 Spread out a different wool, wrap it thinly in the opposite direction, then wet.
3 Continue to wrap the pebble in different colors, wetting them as you go, until the pebble is well covered by at least two complete layers of wool, and all the ends are tucked in.
4 Add silk fibers to form the veining, again wetting with soapy water.
5 Cover the pebble with net and then begin rubbing and felting until the felt feels firm and fits the stone closely.

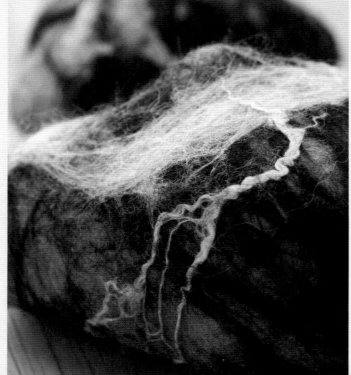

Rocks and minerals display beautiful markings: think of agate and marble.

brown, grey, and black

Glistening, polished fossils; damp, bubbly seaweed; mysterious, earthy fungus; the glowing sun setting over water.

fossils

Cocoons from the silkworm can be successfully trapped into felt by laying a few wool fibers over the top. They will retain their three-dimensional quality and add an unusual texture. The cocoons used in this project are their natural white color, but they can be dyed in vibrant colors.

Materials
1 oz (30 g) black merino wool top
¾ in (2 cm) wide strips of silk fabric in different weaves, in creams and beiges, selected from douppion, crêpe de chine, tussah silk, and chiffon
½ yard x 1 in (50 x 2.5 cm) cream lace trimming
A few white/cream silk fibers
13 silk cocoons, natural color

Method
1 Refer to the instructions for basic feltmaking on pages 8–14. Lay out two layers of black wool.
2 Arrange the silk fabric strips, lace, cocoons, and silk fibers on the surface.
3 Place fine fibers of black wool horizontally across the silks and cocoons, so that they will become trapped during the felting process.
4 Cover the arrangement with net and wet out.
5 Replace the net with plastic and continue through Stages 3, 4, and 5.

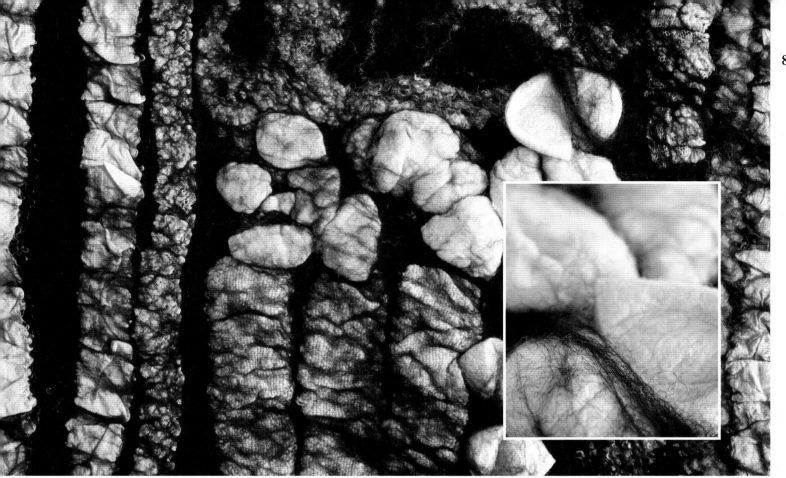

Black and white in contrast; the texture of raw fossils evoked by silk cocoons.

seaweed

The inspiration for this stringy sample of felt was bladderwrack seaweed. Although it could have been made using the network technique on page 20, the holes were actually cut in it at the pre-felt stage, giving the edges a chance to seal at the shrinking stage. To make the bumpy texture, a selection of beans and glass nuggets were tied into the felt after shrinking but before drying. This felt would make an eye-catching and very warm scarf, making either the full length in this way, or just a small piece for decorating the ends.

Materials
⅜ oz (10 g) black/grey merino wool top
⅜ oz (10 g) brown merino wool top
2¼ yd (2 m) novelty yarns with a wool content
10 decorative glass nuggets and dried kidney beans
20 small elastic bands

Method
1 Refer to the instructions for basic feltmaking on pages 8–14, and for making pre-felt on page 16.
2 Make a black pre-felt: lay out two layers of black wool in a longish shape.
3 Make a brown pre-felt: lay out two layers of brown wool in a longish shape.
4 Add the novelty yarns to both pieces, trapping them in place with a few fibers of wool if the yarns do not have much of a wool content.
5 Work both pieces to the pre-felt stage, the end of Stage 3 of basic feltmaking.
6 Cut holes in the pre-felts, making sure that there will be enough solid felt for tying in the glass nuggets.
7 Overlap the pre-felts so that the two colors will felt together into a single piece.
8 Continue the felting to completion, working through Stages 4 and 5, but do not dry.
9 Push the glass nuggets and beans into the reverse of the felt, and secure firmly with tight elastic bands around the base. Leave to dry.
10 When the felt is completely dry, remove the elastic bands. The bumps will remain.

Slithery seaweed, puffed with tiny sacs, translates easily into an exciting piece of felt.

fungus

By using thin plastic resists, layers of felt can be built up. In this piece they were used to give a three-dimensional feel that is reminiscent of bracket fungus. When the felt was dry, tucks were stitched in the back of the bottom layer of felt to add more undulations.

Materials
⅜ oz (30 g) brown, grey-green, and charcoal grey merino wool tops
1⅛ yards (1 m) thick brown/green/black wool yarn

Additional equipment
Plastic (for resist):
2 pieces, about 9¼ x 9¼ in (24 x 24 cm)
1 circle, about 1½ in (4 cm) in diameter

Method
1 Refer to the instructions for basic feltmaking on pages 8–14 and for using a resist on page 31.
2 Lay out two layers of brown wool to make the base. Add some lengths of yarn, extending them beyond the boundaries.
3 Wet out, and cover the base completely with a plastic resist, except for a hole, 7 cm (2¾ in) in diameter, cut in the center.
4 Make the middle, working on top of the base. Lay out two layers of the grey-green wool, slightly inside the base, covering some of the plastic and the center hole.
5 Wet out. Cover with another plastic resist, again with a hole in the center.
6 Make the top, working on top of the middle. Using the charcoal grey wool, lay out another two layers, making them slightly smaller than the middle. This time, place a small circle of plastic in the center. Place wool around the edges of the plastic circle to make an extra ridge. Wet out.
7 Complete the felt by working through Stages 3, 4, and 5 of the basic feltmaking process.
8 When the felt is dry, you can stitch rough tucks in the underside if you wish, to give more shape to the piece. Use loose stitches.

Fungus provides great shapes to inspire a uniquely layered organic piece of felt.

sunset at sea

The shimmering effect of sunlight on water is magical. Here, a strip of metallic fabric has been embedded beneath the top layer of wool and has ruched on shrinking, emulating the ripples on the water. Lustrous silk fibers in glowing red and orange, and soft, creamy white, paint the sunset and provide a contrast with the matte surface of the wool.

Materials

½ oz (15 g) dark grey merino wool top
½ oz (15 g) navy merino wool top
12 x 2 in (30 x 5 cm) gold metallic
   fabric (fairly open weave)
Small quantity silk fibers in rich red,
   orange, and white

Method

1 Refer to the instructions for basic feltmaking on pages 8–14, and for adding fabrics and fibers to felt on page 18.
2 Lay out a layer of grey wool.
3 Lay out a layer of navy wool on top of this, placing the fibers at right angles to those in the grey layer.
4 Position the strip of gold fabric, trapping it in place with wisps of navy wool.
5 Arrange the silk fibers, loosely striping the orange and red across the top, and making amorphous shapes with the white further down.
6 Cover with net and wet out, working through Stages 2, 3, 4, and 5 to complete the felt.

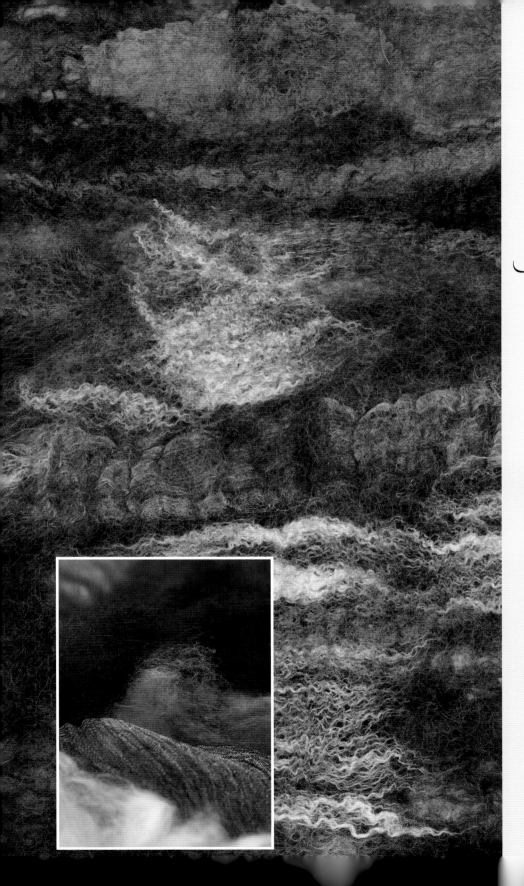

The last flash of glorious color before sky and sea blend into darkness.

recycled

Bits of old knitting; vibrant wrappers; luxuriant Indian saris.

knitting

To make this piece, scraps of fabric were machine-stitched to a moth-eaten wool sweater before shrinking it in the washing machine. A small amount of dry wool was placed under some of the fabrics before the stitching, in order to create a shape. This is a good opportunity to be experimental: try different weights of fabric, natural and synthetic.

Materials

15¾ x 15¾ in (40 x 40 cm) piece of woollen knitting
2¾ x 2¾ in (7 x 7 cm) scraps of silk fabric and
  silk velvet
4 strips, 15¾ x ¾ in (40 x 2 cm) velvet
Tiny quantity merino wool top in a color to match
Machine thread

Method

1 Arrange the squares of fabric on the knitting and pin in place. Pin out flat: the squares will distort as the wool shrinks.
2 Place a small amount of wool under some of the squares.
3 Using a zigzag stitch, machine-stitch the fabrics in place around the edges.
4 Place a velvet strip near each edge of the knitting and machine-stitch in place with a zigzag stitch.
5 Cut holes out of the knitting, between the squares.
6 Put into the washing machine on a hot cycle with a fast spin. Dry.

Knitted garments and
scraps of material
reinvented and given a
new lease on life.

wrappers

Never throw anything away! The net bags that oranges are sold in, together with colored foil and cellophane candy wrappers, can be incorporated into a piece of felt with a little care. The net's grid-like structure will need to have wool fibers on either side to trap it, as the net is too slippery to adhere by itself. Alternatively, weave a little wool through the net before adding it to the base layer.

Materials
⅜ oz (10 g) in total of turquoise, orange, and lime merino wool tops
3 net fruit bags, each a different color
6 foil or cellophane candy wrappers

Method
1 Refer to the instructions for basic feltmaking on pages 8–14, and for adding fabrics and fibers to felt on page 18.
2 Lay out the three colors of wool in three wide stripes. Lay out a second layer.
3 Smooth out the candy wrappers and arrange them on each block of color.
4 Place a piece of fruit net over each candy wrapper and cover with a few wisps of wool in the appropriate color.
5 Complete Stage 1 of basic feltmaking by covering the arrangement with net, then continue through Stages 2, 3, 4, and 5.
6 When the felt is dry, it could be further embellished if you wish.

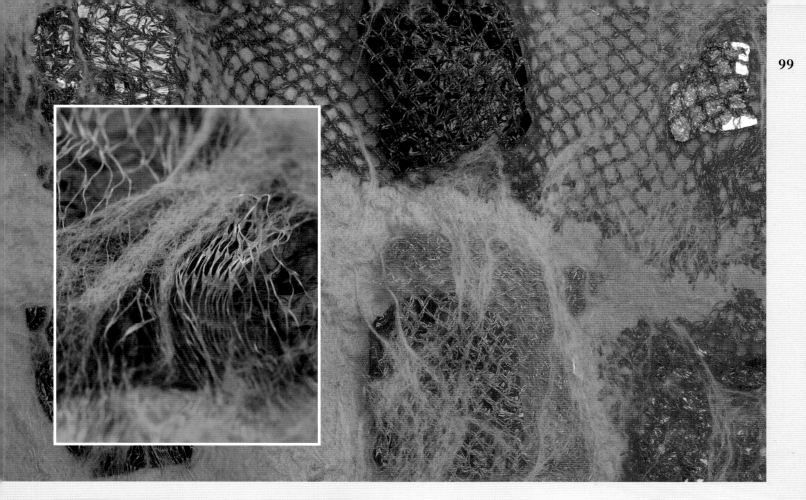

Create a truly exuberant surface from everyday objects. The colors speak of sunny citrus groves.

saris

Printed fabrics take on a new look when incorporated into felt. Choose fabrics that are of a slightly open weave, made of natural fibers if possible, because these will felt in most successfully. Old scarves of chiffon or silk, blouses and dresses in fine cotton, rayon, or silk all work well. Silk saris often have several patterns in a single length, so they're especially beautiful to use, and the silk makes a crunchy texture when shrunk.

Materials

1 oz (30 g) purple merino wool top
3 pieces printed fabric in silk and rayon,
   each 12 x 4 in (30 x 10 cm)

Method

1 Refer to the instructions for basic feltmaking on pages 8–14, and for adding fabrics and fibers to felt on page 18.
2 Lay out two layers of wool.
3 Cut or tear the pieces of fabric into wavy-edged strips; the rough edges will help the material to felt in.
4 Arrange the fabrics on the wool.
5 Cover with net, then continue through Stages 2, 3, 4, and 5 of basic feltmaking.

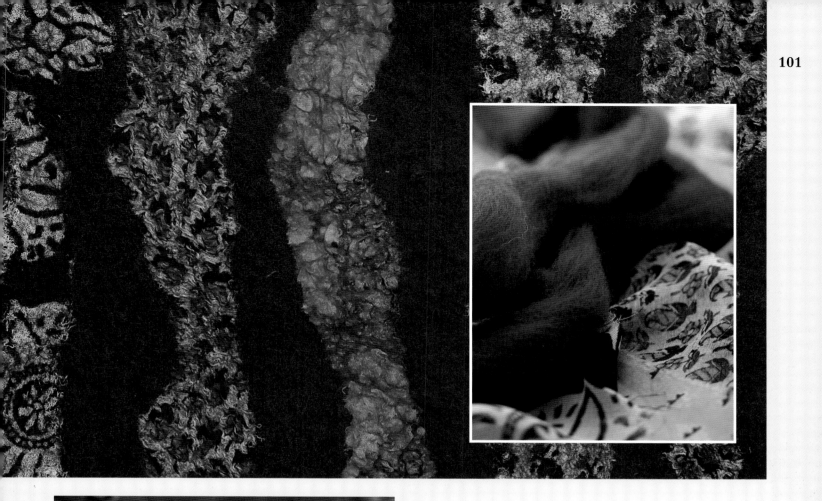

Fragile silks blend into the inky purple of an Indian night sky: a rich tapestry of color.

fun
things

An alien cactus; a snaking tangle of quayside color; striking, unusual jewels.

cactus

You can use this technique to make a delightful addition for the top of a hat, or for the bottom or front of a bag. The spikes can be as long as you want. They can be knotted, plaited, woven, or have beads threaded on them. Another idea is to cover the surface of a piece of felt with very short, thin spikes. You can have lots of fun with this technique.

Materials
¾ oz (20 g) dark green merino wool top
Tiny quantity merino wool top for each
  spike, various colors

Method
1 Refer to the instructions for basic feltmaking on pages 8–14, and for making spikes on page 22.
2 Make as many spikes as you want.
3 Make the background. Lay out two layers of green wool.
4 Plant the dry ends of the spikes on the green wool, as close together as you can.
5 Lay green wool over and around the roots of the spikes, wetting out and pressing firmly.
6 Cover with plastic sheeting, and pull the spikes through a hole cut in the middle. The spikes should flop in all directions.
7 Continue through Stages 4 and 5 of basic feltmaking.

Unearthly spikes burst
out of the ground — and
a rainbow-colored cactus
comes to life.

fishing net

Fishing paraphernalia lying on a windswept dock is a picture postcard sight. This project looks complicated but it is actually very easy to do, using the techniques for network felt and cords. Because the cords are shrunk fully before the ends are attached, they will twist and loop around the network.

Materials
¾ oz (20 g) in total of merino wool tops in assorted colors, for the network
⅜ oz (10 g) in total of merino wool tops in contrasting colors, for the cords

Method
1 Refer to the instructions for basic feltmaking on pages 8–14, network felt on page 20, and cords on page 21.
2 Lay out the wool for the network of fleece.
3 Complete Stages 2 and 3 of basic feltmaking – wetting out, covering with net and felting.
4 Make the cords, but leave both ends dry.
5 Weave the cords randomly through the holes in the network, spreading their dry ends on the wrong side of the network so that they will felt into the underside of the piece. Felt them in following the instructions for spikes on page 22.
6 Complete the felt by working through Stages 4 and 5 of basic feltmaking.

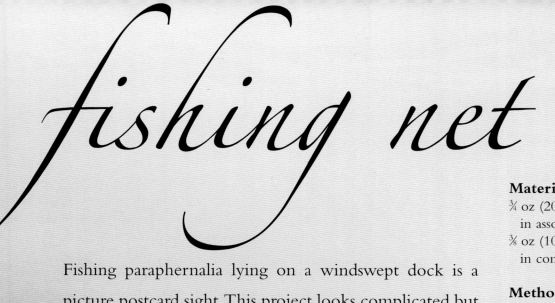

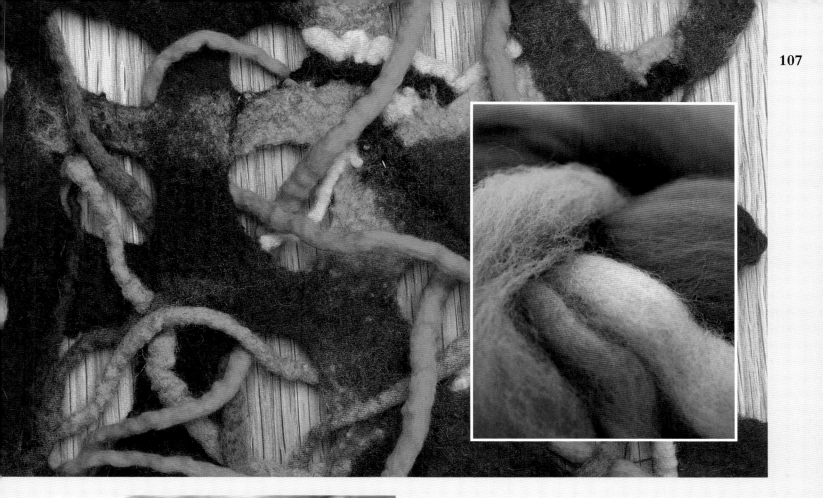

A jumble of fishing
nets and ropes realized
as twisting spirals on a
bold honeycomb.

bangles

Textile jewelry adds an idiosyncratic touch to whatever you are wearing. You can use felt to make bangles, brooches, corsages, and bobbles, and embellish it with tiny beads and sequins, if you want. Bobbles (see page 23) can be made into beads, buttons, and earrings. Here is how to make a bangle.

Materials
½ oz (15 g) per bangle of merino wool top, in
  a color, or various colors, of your choice
1⅛ yd (1 m) novelty wool yarn
Beads for embellishment

Method
1 Refer to the instructions for making cords on page 21. Take a length of wool and wrap it fairly loosely over your hand, around the palm. This will make a bangle of the appropriate size.
2 Wet it with a small amount of hot, soapy water and massage the wool, moving it around your hand and making it into a cord with the ends joined to make a circle.
3 Remove the felt from your hand. Take another length of wool and wrap it round and round the bangle, threading it through the centre each time. Continue until the bangle reaches the desired thickness.
4 Twist the yarn around the felt, threading it through the center of the bangle.
5 Continue massaging the wool and rubbing the bangle on the bubble wrap until the yarn has felted in and the bangle feels very firm. Rinse and leave to dry.
6 Embellish with beads as desired.

Make a splash with one-off pieces of jewelry to treasure and be proud of.

glossary

Appliqué A technique in which small shapes are cut from a material, or materials, and applied to a base material. Felt appliqué consists of making pieces of pre-felt and applying them to a base of pre-felt.

Blending Using carders to blend different colors of wool before starting the feltmaking process. This process can be used to create interesting effects.

Carded wool Wool that has been cleaned and processed by machine. It is presented as a mass of loose fibers and is available in a range of natural colors.

Carders Hand carders are brush-like implements consisting of a flat piece of wood covered in metal spikes or 'teeth', with a handle. They are used to blend wool. A tuft of wool is placed on the teeth of one carder, then brushed with the other carder to blend the wool fibers. This process is repeated until the desired effect is obtained. Drum carders are small, hand-operated machines with two rollers covered in teeth, which engage to blend the wool.

Cobweb felt A very soft, fine, and delicate felt resembling a cobweb.

Felt lace See network felt.

Fibers Natural or synthetic filaments, or strands, which can be spun into a yarn.

Flax Plant used to make linen, a natural fiber.

Fleece The woolly coat of a sheep. The raw fleece is processed into carded wool or wool top. Some feltmakers tend to refer to all the wool they use as 'fleece' when it is in fact processed wool.

Fulling Stage 4 of the basic feltmaking process, when the wet wool is shrunk by rolling it.

Georgette A thin, filmy fabric with a crêpe-like appearance.

Merino A breed of sheep reared in Australia, New Zealand, and South Africa. Merino wool is the easiest type to turn into felt.

Mosaic In feltmaking, this is a technique where individual pieces of pre-felt are arranged in a design and then bonded into a single piece by easing their edges together. The joined edges can be reinforced with strands of wool on the reverse of the piece.

Natural fibers/fabrics Fibers from entirely natural sources, such as silk from the silkworm, cotton from the cotton plant, or wool from sheep. Natural fabrics are made from natural fibers that do not undergo any chemical changes during conversion to fabric.

Network felt Also known as felt lace. Felt featuring a network of holes.

Pilling General wear and tear on a wool garment can cause it to pill – form tiny balls of wool on the surface.

Positive and negative inlay A technique where two pieces of pre-felt are made, then an identical shape is cut out of each. The removed shape from one piece of pre-felt is inserted into the hole in the other piece of pre-felt, which it fits exactly.

Pre-felt Felt that is not fully finished. The wool fibers have been worked to the stage where they begin to mat together, but the shrinking process has not been carried out (i.e. to the end of Stage 3, felting, of basic feltmaking). Pre-felt is used for techniques such as mosaic and appliquéing. Sometimes pre-felt is used wet; sometimes it is used dry, for example when you want to incorporate stitchwork into individual pieces of pre-felt before using them further in a felt work.

Rayon A man-made fiber created from cellulose such as wood or cotton.

Resist A resist is similar to a template, in that it is used to create a certain shape. However it also prevents the wool that is laid over it from adhering to the wool underneath during the felting process. This is useful if you want to make a flap or a tuck. The resist is made of a piece of thin plastic cut into the shape of the flap.

Silk fabric Woven silk fabric, on a roll, that you buy by the yard. There are many different types, ranging from fine and smooth to heavy and textured. Some names you may come across are silk noil, tussah silk, and douppion silk.

Silk fibers Individual fibers of silk, which can be bought in many different forms. They are available in richly dyed colors, as well as natural shades. For example, there is silk thread for machine or hand embroidery, silk tops, and silk waste. You could also fray fibers from a piece of woven silk fabric yourself.

Silk tops Silk fibers that have been prepared and combed ready for use.

Silk waste Waste resulting from the production of silk and from the weaving industry. In the past silk waste would have been thrown away, but now it is recycled to be used by textile artists.

Template A shape used as a master pattern for replicating that shape. In feltmaking, templates made from plastic foam flooring underlay are easy to use and produce good results. You could also use pliable plastic or even bubble wrap, although the latter is not as strong.

Wetting out Stage 2 of the basic feltmaking process: the wool fibers are covered with a piece of net, soapy water is added, and the fibers are made thoroughly wet. The net is then replaced with a piece of plastic sheeting.

Wool top Wool that has been cleaned, processed, and dyed, then combed and formed into a long, soft rope.

index

Entries & page numbers in *italics* indicate projects

acknowledgments

Editor **Lisa John**
Executive Art Editor **Leigh Jones**
Designer **Jo Tapper**
Photographer **Vanessa Davies**
Illustrator **Sheilagh Noble**
Production Manager **Simone Nauerth**

Picture Acknowledgements
Special photography:
© Octopus Publishing Group Ltd/Vanessa Davies
Other photography:
Alamy/Tim Hill 72; **Corbis**/Robert Pickett 80;
Getty Images/Freddy Storheil 68; **Leigh Jones** 56, 74, 104;
Lizzie Houghton 38, 40, 60, 62, 63, 90, 92, 106;
Octopus Publishing Group Limited 36, 64; **PhotoDisc** 48.